Focus On

Adults

. . . .

A Handbook for Teachers

by William P. Campbell

Gospel Publishing House
Springfield, Missouri
02–0407

Library of Congress Catalog Card Number 93–078162
International Standard Book Number 0–88243–407–1
Printed in the United States of America

Contents

The Ministry Of Teaching Adults

Teaching is at the heart of ministry, it was Jesus' passion. As one writer noted, "He was often a healer, sometimes a worker of miracles, frequently a preacher, but always a teacher."[1] Christ's parting words were a call to continue the ministry of teaching. "Go and make disciples of all nations...teaching them to obey everything I have commanded you" (Matthew 28:19,20). This commission establishes teaching as the primary function of the Church.

In Acts 2 we find Spirit-filled adults learning together from the apostles, "continuing in their doctrine." In the great persecution (Acts 8) these educated adults spread the apostles' teachings throughout the Mediterranean world. In Acts 18, team-teachers Priscilla and Aquila explained to Apollos the way of God more adequately. The Colossians learned God's truth from Epaphras (Colossians 1:7). The ceaseless chain reaction had begun.

Paul's charge to pastors and teachers was to "prepare God's people for works of service" (Ephesians 4:12). The adult Sunday school provides the forum to fulfill this task. Writing to Timothy, Paul said, "the things you have heard me say in the presence of many witnesses entrust to reliable men who will also be qualified to teach others" (2 Timothy 2:2). Adults teaching adults to teach adults is the pattern that has carried the Church through the ages to this present day.

THE GOALS OF CHRISTIAN EDUCATION

Three Landmarks for Christian Educators

In the early years of maritime navigation, sighting a particular star or coastline landmark was useful to maintain a proper course. Teachers also must guard against wandering off course, of drifting aimlessly in a sea of busyness. Have you ever felt your work was pointless or without direction? Such drifting means we have lost sight of our landmarks. We can regain our sense of direction by looking for landmarks in the Word. The process of "making disciples" (Matthew 28:19,20) and "building up the body" (Ephesians 4:12,13) present the three landmarks of Sunday school work: evangelism, education, and edification.

Evangelism

Unsaved men and women will be in your class, brought by friends, a Christian child, or perhaps as a result of your church's visitation program. This opportunity to introduce them to the message of God's Word is what Sunday school is all about. The Spirit can use you to bring searching people to Christ.

Education

Losing sight of education is what causes many classes to deteriorate into an hour of aimless conversation on Sunday morning. A dictionary definition of *education* is the process of training and developing knowledge, skill, mind, and character. Because it is a *process* we should not expect results overnight. A Sunday school teacher needs patience!

Edification

Edification is "the act of building" used figuratively in the New Testament of promoting spiritual growth and well-being. "Therefore encourage one another and build each other up" (1 Thessalonians 5:11). Edification focuses on the heart, while education focuses on the mind. We need not only knowledge (education), but also love (edification). "Knowledge puffs up, but love builds up" (1 Corinthians 8:1). We want both knowledge and love working together. Love helps us discern the beneficial and constructive use of knowledge (1 Corinthians 10:23,24).

A Sunday school teacher must periodically ask, "Does my teaching seek to strengthen the spiritual life of my students? Am I challenging my students to think, to exercise their minds by considering new points of view? Am I helping them to build meaningful relationships within the class?" Evangelism, education, and edification are the landmarks to keep our ministry on course.

The Ultimate Goal of All Believers—Maturity

Every teacher should be familiar with Ephesians 4:11–16. It indicates that Church leaders are to equip believers so that they, in turn, can do works of service and build up the body of Christ. This is to continue until we all reach maturity, defined as the whole measure of the fullness of Christ. Maturity summarizes the biblical goals of teaching. But when looking at your students, how do you measure maturity? Michael Lawson suggests four scriptural themes that summarize the idea of biblical maturity.[2]

1. Love

Jesus replied: "'Love the Lord your God with all your heart and with all your soul and with all your mind.' This is the first and greatest commandment. And the second is like it: 'Love your neighbor as yourself.'" (Matthew 22:37–39.)

Teaching is to produce love in the student's life. The command to love ties together a great deal of the New Testament and Christ's teachings. Until a student produces love, the task of teaching is not complete. "By this all men will know that you are my disciples, if you love one another" (John 13:35). "What is love?" is answered in behavioral terms in 1 Corinthians 13.

2. Morality

"But solid food is for the mature, who by constant use have trained themselves to distinguish good from evil" (Hebrews

5:14). The mature disciple is (1) able to take "solid food," and (2) able to distinguish between good and evil because he has developed his moral senses. We have not reached the goal of adult Christian education until students are consistently making correct moral choices. Making good choices requires practice (Philippians 3:12–14).

3. Theological Stability

"No longer be infants, tossed back and forth by the waves, and blown here and there by every wind of teaching and by the cunning craftiness of men in their deceitful scheming" (Ephesians 4:14). Maturity is measured by theological stability. This coincides with Hebrews 5:14 which suggests that mature believers are able to deal with solid food.

4. Christian Service

Teachers are to assist in the preparation of God's people for "works of service, so that the body of Christ may be built up" (Ephesians 4:12). Christian service is a by-product of Christian education. We are taught to serve. Willingness to serve is evidence of growing maturity. Adult Christian education helps people to discover their God-given gifts and to use them in meaningful service.

THE SPIRITUAL GROWTH PROCESS

Learning is not a changed nature, but it is changed behavior. The difference is important. We do not learn in order to enter God's kingdom. Education cannot save us, only acceptance of Christ's work on Calvary can do that. Learning changes us to right behavior within God's kingdom. It is the changing of our skills, our attitudes, and our actions. Learning for the Christian is exercising the fruit of the Spirit (Galatians 5:22,23) and growing in Christ-likeness. It is continuous growth involving our knowledge, our feelings, our actions, and our relationships. Learning calls for change.

"I urge you, brothers,...Do not conform any longer to the pattern of this world, but be transformed by the renewing of your mind" (Romans 12:2).

Spiritual growth takes place through the work of the indwelling Holy Spirit as the individual makes conscious use of his will and his mind. Learning and spiritual growth, while not the same, do go hand in hand.

Colossians 1:9–10 helps us to see the relationship between learning and spiritual growth. It has been referred to as the Colossians cycle because it points out the ongoing and cyclical process of spiritual growth.

"We have not stopped praying for you and asking God to fill you with the knowledge of his will through all spiritual wisdom and understanding. And we pray this in order that you may live a life worthy of the Lord and may please him in every way: bearing fruit in every good work, growing in the knowledge of God" (Colossians 1:9–10.)

The cycle of spiritual growth is outlined in five steps:

1. Bible—"Knowledge of what God has willed." Our teaching starts with God's Word. This is where students come to gain the knowledge they need to begin the process.

2. Life-implications—"Spiritual wisdom and understanding." Here the Holy Spirit illuminates the mind to see the personal implications of God's truth. The teacher plays a critical role in this as he relates God's Word to the student's life experience. He is answering the student's "so-what?" about the lesson.

3. Response—"Live a life worthy of the Lord." Here the student acts upon his new understanding of God's will, he begins to obey. "Therefore everyone who hears these words of mine and puts them into practice is like a wise man who built his house on the rock. The rain came down, the streams rose, and the winds

blew and beat against that house; yet it did not fall, because it had its foundation on the rock" (Matthew 7:24–25).

4. Fruit—"Bearing fruit in every good work." This fruit is the practical benefit of living in harmony with God, but also the work of the Holy Spirit reproducing His character within us evidenced by the fruit of the Spirit (Galatians 5:22,23). Fruitfulness is also reflected in Christian service and Christian life-style.

5. Knowing God Better—"Increasing in the knowledge of God." Life in Christ brings a growing personal knowledge of God. We have progressed from knowing about Him to knowing Him. Of course, this brings further insights and comprehension of God's Word, thus restarting the cycle. This explains the common experience of reading a familiar portion of Scripture and suddenly perceiving truths and insights we had never seen before.

THE TEACHER AND THE LEARNING PROCESS

The life and personality of a teacher have a significant influence on student learning. We are speaking of the interpersonal dynamics between a teacher and a student, and how the student perceives the teacher as an individual. In other words, how you relate personally (person to person) is as influential as how you relate positionally (teacher to student).

We can enhance the teacher-student relationship by understanding the characteristics and needs of adults in their various stages of development. We should also know the individual adult as a person. It may be helpful to keep a student information file containing the name, address, telephone number, date of birth, spouse's name, occupation, and children's names. It also may be helpful to include when the student accepted Christ, when he or she was filled with the Spirit, what church and community activities he or she participates in, what hobbies, interests, and special talents he or she has.

Any teacher-student relationship can be enriched by personal contacts outside the classroom. Letter or phone contacts when the student is sick is standard teacher practice. Visit him in his home, not often but often enough to let him know you care. If your motivation is to build a relationship and express love and concern, such contacts will be genuine and well received.

In a real sense, you are a pastor or shepherd to your students. Your responsibilities to them are very much like your pastor's responsibilities to the congregation. Your students need similar care from you. The teacher-student relationship will affect your success as a teacher more than any other single factor.

THE HOLY SPIRIT AND THE LEARNING PROCESS

God's role in the teaching ministry can be distorted two ways. One is to discount it, saying God has nothing to do with it. The other is to make God's role a magical thing, demanding that God work against all natural processes or participation by man. However, the apostle Paul recognized a wonderful and mysterious sharing of responsibility. He said, "I planted the seed, Apollos watered it, but God made it grow" (1 Corinthians 3:6). God's divine working accompanies human effort, it is not a substitute for it.

It is best to realize that, ordinarily, God works through natural means in a supernatural way. Just as a farmer's study of agriculture does not make God unnecessary, so a teacher's study of educational theory and teaching techniques is not choosing the natural over the supernatural. In both instances, our human efforts just allow us to cooperate more intelligently with God, enabling God to bring forth a greater harvest.

What we want to do is cooperate with God more intelligently in the area of Christian education. When we apply our best skills to the teaching ministry we become a type of catalyst helping to bring about a reaction between the Holy Spirit and the student. God can use teachers to help perfect the relationship between the pupil and God.

This requires teachers to seek the Holy Spirit's help; we must be anointed to teach. The anointing is the Spirit's enablement to communicate truth effectively. The apostle Paul said of his preaching and teaching, "The Holy Spirit's power was in my words, proving to those who heard them that the message was from God" (1 Corinthians 2:4, *The Living Bible*).

So we see the teacher maintain a two-fold dependency: a need for knowledgeable and skillful human effort, while yielding to and trusting in God's supernatural accomplishing of the task.

THE STUDENT AND THE LEARNING PROCESS

Motivation is the key to learning, it is what brings learning to changed behavior. We must understand adult motivation. We cannot motivate anyone. We can only create an environment that cultivates a student's own motivation.

Students learn spiritual truth in the context of human relationships (family, marriage, church, interaction). Encourage the students to build these types of relationships.

How is Christian education different from secular education? Unique content is part of it. But the unique context of loving relationships is what sets it apart (John 13:35). Love motivates and loving relationships enhance spiritual development. It is a myth that adults attend Sunday school primarily to learn. Adults attend Sunday school for the fellowship, caring, and support they can give and receive. Caring relationships are the setting for learning and for spiritual growth.

TEACHING—GIVING THE LIGHT OF KNOWLEDGE

"For God, who said, 'Let light shine out of darkness,' made his light shine in our hearts to give us the light of the knowledge of the glory of God in the face of Christ. But we have this treasure in jars of clay to show that this all-surpassing power is from God and not from us." (2 Corinthians 4:6–7)

A teacher has no greater joy, no greater sense of ministry, than when a student's spiritual eyes are opened, whether that be for the first time at salvation or subsequently gaining deeper insights into the truths of God's Word. Teaching is a ministry of working with the Holy Spirit to bring spiritual understanding to the student.

We see this mission highlighted in two Scripture passages. First, the Parable of the Sower in Matthew 13:1–23. It is easy to identify with the sower. Just as the sower walked across the field broadcasting the seed with arm-sweeping motions, so the teacher disperses God's Word to his students.

It is almost impossible, at that moment, to know whether or not you are meeting with success. That evaluation requires time, the soil will tell the tale. In the parable there were four soil types: the hard-packed soil of the path, the shallow soil upon the rocks, the thorny ground, and the good soil. Each represents various responses to the gospel.

The crucial difference between gospel seed that is snatched away and that which produces a generous yield is explained in verses 19 and 23. In the former, the person hearing the Word "does not understand." In the latter he does understand. Understanding is the key! First and foremost, a Sunday school teacher must help the student understand the Word.

Consider also the incident of Philip and the Ethiopian eunuch (Acts 8:26–35). The Ethiopian was troubled by his inability to understand a passage in Isaiah. Philip asked him, "Do you understand what you are reading?" The African official replied, "How can I unless someone explains it to me?" Again we see the teacher's crucial role as one who brings understanding.

The pilgrim asked, "Tell me, please, who is the prophet talking about, himself or someone else?" Teachers are sometimes more comfortable asking questions than answering them. But students need to be given opportunity to ask questions, to express what they are curious about.

Philip's response to the eunuch's question provides an excellent model for the Sunday school teacher. "Then Philip began with that very passage of Scripture and told him the good news about Jesus" (verse 35). The teacher began the learning process at the student's point of interest and understanding, then led him to a greater understanding of the good news about Jesus. This is the ministry of teaching!

The Science of Teaching Adults

The word *pedagogy* is defined as "the art, science, or profession of teaching."[3] The word literally means "child leading" and comes from an ancient Greek name given to a slave responsible for escorting his master's children to and from school and assisting them with their education. Until recently the word was used of teaching in general.

Today, educators are beginning to distinguish between child and adult learning. Pedagogy now refers specifically to helping children learn; while a new term, *andragogy* (based on the Greek word *aner* for man) is now used for the art and science of helping adults learn. This has come about because of a growing realization that adults do not approach learning in the same way as children. The apostle Paul expressed this very idea: "When I was a child, I talked like a child, I thought like a child, I reasoned like a child. When I became a man, I put childish ways behind me" (1 Corinthians 13:11).

THE ADULT APPROACH TO LEARNING

Advocates of andragogy offer four assumptions about adults that distinguish them from children. One, as an individual matures their self-concept moves from being a dependent personality toward being a self-directed human being. Two, as individuals mature they accumulate a reservoir of experiences that become a growing resource for learning. Three, as individuals mature their readiness to learn becomes oriented more to the developmental tasks of their social roles. And four, as individuals mature their time perspective changes from one of postponed to immediate application of knowledge.[4] These observations make adult learning experiences and motivation very different from that of children.

1. Adults are more self-directed in their learning.

In childhood, the teacher decides what, when, and how the child will learn. But adults see themselves as self-directed and expect others to view them that way also. Adults want to decide for themselves what they will learn, when they will learn it, and how they will go about it. The teacher and adult student see each other as equals in a mutually helpful relationship.

2. Adult learning goals are specific and more immediate.

Children go to school to gain a broad understanding of subjects that will help them later in life. Their studies are one of postponed application. They are told, "someday you'll need to know that." Adults have a much different time perspective. They read a book or enroll in a course looking for answers to specific problems, and they want to make immediate applications. We could say the child's learning is *subject-centered*, while the adult's learning is *problem-centered*.

3. An adult's greater life-experience is an important aid in learning.

In childhood, the teacher's experience is the primary resource for learning. A child's experience is considered of relatively little worth. This makes the child very dependent on the teacher, and the learning situation is characterized more by one-way communication.

But for adults, everyone's experience and knowledge is valued as a resource. Adults share their knowledge, and as a result everyone's learning is enriched; the teacher is not the sole contributor. Adults are more interdependent in their learning with multidirectional communication.

4. Adults group themselves for learning more on the basis of interest than on the basis of age-level.

For children, decisions about grouping and curriculum are based strictly on age. Certain subjects are deemed appropriate at a certain age. Adults are not as concerned about age, they gravitate toward those with similar concerns and interests. For example, a community education course on household maintenance or a church class on enriching your marriage are likely to have adults of a wide age-span. It is not the age but the subject that is important.

FACTORS THAT INFLUENCE ADULT LEARNING

1. Aging and the Mind

Today we understand the old saying "You can't teach an old dog new tricks" as a myth. However, the process of aging does affect learning throughout the adult years.

A person's *general intelligence* is composed of two elements technically referred to as "fluid" intelligence and "crystallized" intelligence. Fluid intelligence is biologically or genetically determined. We can refer to this mental horsepower as *natural intelligence.* Crystallized intelligence is altered by education and experience. In other words, a person's intelligence can be cultivated and nourished. We can refer to this as *nurtured intelligence.*

Both aspects of intelligence increase from birth through adolescence, but then natural intelligence begins gradually to decline with age. Nurtured intelligence, on the other hand, continues to increase with more life experience and education. The net effect is that the loss in natural intelligence is offset by the gains in nurtured intelligence. General intelligence remains basically stable.

Performance in different tasks differs with age. For example, younger adults generally learn more quickly, memorization is easy. However, they are not as well-equipped to apply new knowledge to life as are older adults. They do not have the background, the experience, and the education to effectively integrate learning with life. Older adults, on the other hand, may take longer to memorize information, or to master a skill. However, they can more quickly and more accurately apply new learning to life. If older adults are able to control the pace of their learning, their ability to learn is significant. For these reasons, rushing adults can be nonproductive. The pace of learning and the amount of time given to discuss and master new material is important. Giving adults adequate time to complete their learning increases their confidence.

2. Aging and the Body

Throughout the middle adult years the aging process makes itself known. The most not able aspects of physical aging on learning are eyesight and hearing. Almost like clockwork, many adults begin to notice vision difficulties at 40 years of age. As one becomes older the field of vision narrows and the eyes take longer to adapt to the dark.

Hearing is certainly important for learning in classroom situations. As men age they lose their capacity to hear higher tones, while women lose the capacity to hear lower tones. Hearing loss contributes to the loss of accuracy in information received, the loss of self-confidence and security, and even a change in personal relationships. If an adult responds to a misinterpreted question, the resulting answer may trigger amazement or amusement from the class. An embarrassing incident like this may cause withdrawal from participation in the future. Rapid speech may cause an older adult to experience a 45 percent loss of intelligibility.

3. Previous Education

Adults enter learning situations with a whole set of attitudes from previous experiences. If those experiences were negative, if they were embarrassed or rebuked for example, they will be reluctant to approach anything that looks like a classroom.

However, positive experiences will correspondingly bring positive feeling about education. This adult will welcome new learning and he will be eager to join in the church's programs.

Knowing the amount of formal education an adult has been involved in, and what his experiences were like can explain a great deal about his willingness or unwillingness to become involved in the church's Christian education ministries. Generally, the more formal education a person has had the more likely he will enjoy a structured classroom setting. A high-school dropout, or someone who did poorly in school may not. Keep in mind that adults will respond differently to different types of programs and educational settings.

4. Personality

An individual's personality can also affect his approach to learning. How we believe others view us influences how we view ourselves. Feelings of hopelessness, alienation, defensiveness, loneliness, or shyness will discourage adults from trying something new. This is why adults will respond differently to various teaching methods and participation activities. A wise teacher will take personality into account when dealing with adults.

5. Motivation

It is very unnerving to stand before a class of what appears to be disinterested and apathetic adults. But beyond the possible damage to a teacher's self-esteem is the danger that adult Christian education has come to a halt. Lack of motivation should be an urgent concern because people learn more effectively if they are motivated to learn.

Be as concerned about motivating students as you are about informing them. After all, our ultimate goal is not merely to deliver God's truth but to motivate adults to study God's Word for themselves—to inspire them to press on in learning and spiritual growth.

Principles For Adult Christian Education[5]

We have discussed how adults approach learning. Let's summarize this by looking at some principles that can help us work effectively with adults.

Adults learn best when they are treated with respect

As James DeBoy observes, "Children realize that they are dependent on others for many aspects of their lives. However, adults see themselves as self-directing individuals who are independent. If adults perceive that they are being treated as children or without respect (being talked down to or given simplistic explanations, with their questions ridiculed or ignored) they will not participate in such programs."

Adults Are Motivated When Allowed To Make Decisions

Being self-directed, adults appreciate being allowed to make decisions and choices. When adults have input they will have interest. Give them support and guidance, but let them have the room to succeed and make mistakes. Apply this principle in your class by allowing adults to sit where they want, by letting them help select the topics of study, and give them the responsibility to plan social events.

Adults Learn Best When Physically Comfortable

Children can tolerate uncomfortable situations better than adults; of course, children deserve the best conditions possible. But adults have little tolerance for discomfort. The physical effects of aging inflict adults with a greater sensitivity. Muscles cramp and joints stiffen more easily. They get chilled or overheated. Extraneous noises can distract them. They need conditions consistent with their hearing and vision needs. Poor ventilation can cause drowsiness. Adults also have much higher expectations than children. They are accustomed to quality treatment in the secular community, and expect the same in the church. Uncomfortable surroundings will hinder adult learning.

Adults Learn Best When They Feel Accepted

The more the teacher does to build relationships with the students and between students the more relaxed adults will be, and the more they will learn. Just as being a pastor has an element of teaching in it, so teaching a Sunday school class has an element of pastoral ministry. Spending time with adults, and carefully listening to them will help them feel accepted. The sharing of burdens in prayer will also help bond the class together. Give opportunity for adults to react, question, and comment. If necessary, use small group techniques to do this. Adults also respond well to talking informally over light refreshments. Comfortable settings and fellowship are not just "nice things to do," they are essential in adult Christian education.

Adults Are Motivated By A Sense Of Accomplishment

Ease brings boredom, and adults are probably the most under challenged students in the Sunday school. Yet people feel best when they succeed in those things that challenge them, such as, getting a driver's license, earning a college degree, losing 40 pounds, or mastering a craft.

Have your students assist you in the lesson presentation. Have them prepare a special learning project. One adult class made a handwritten Bible for the church library. They had a great sense of accomplishment and learned at the same time. Give them a challenge. You may even consider some testing on a particular subject. This could be done before and after a lesson series to show them how much they have learned.

Adults Are Motivated When The Teacher Is Excited

Excitement breeds excitement. Enthusiasm is not necessarily shouting or jumping up and down. It can be communicated by simply being early to class or by having a well-prepared lesson. Let them see that you believe what you are doing is important. Be joyful and generally excited about teaching. Live your faith in and out of the classroom.

Adults Are Motivated When They Can See Immediate Rewards For The Time Invested

Time is valuable to adults; they do not want to waste it! Studies on the lack of adult participation in secular learning opportunities showed the greatest reasons to be lack of time and scheduling problems.[6] Many adults would respond similarly about participation in various Christian education programs.

The Christian education program must be worthwhile. If adults can see the benefits of learning, they will be much more inclined to participate. To encourage adult participation show them how the class (seminar, retreat, workshop, etc.) will help them personally (grow in their faith) or functionally (help them be a better parent, handle money better, etc.). Make clear what they will gain by the study. And when preparing lessons, write as effective and practical lesson objectives as possible.

Adults Usually Have A Problem-Centered Rather Than Subject-Centered Motivation To Learn

Adults are motivated by practical concerns. When left to themselves, adults initiate learning to solve a problem, to answer a question, or to solve a puzzle. If an adult wants to know how to do home repair, to catch a bass, to sew a dress, to use a computer, or to do anything else, he or she will read a book, attend a class, ask a knowledgeable friend, or find some other means to learn. The point is adults are motivated to learn, so they do learn.

Know your students' interests. What are the questions, problems and needs that concern them? Adult learning does not take place in a vacuum. Life experiences dominate adult's thinking, and they approach learning in response to issues that confront them. This is why "how-to" books and seminars do so well, adults respond to their problem-solving orientation. Work hard to orient your lessons toward problem-solving with biblical solutions. Bible stories without life-related emphasis have little meaning to adults. Your challenge is to bridge the gap between Bible content and life application.

Adults Are Motivated To Learn How To Cope With Social Roles And Developmental Tasks

Every adult has certain roles to play in life (e.g., spouse, parent, friend, or worker) and faces various developmental tasks (e.g., selecting a mate, rearing children, managing a home, finding a job, adjusting to the death of a loved one, and retirement). These involve a certain readiness to learn or a "teachable moment." Adult learning programs should be timed to coincide with adult motivation coming from these teachable moments.

Newly married couples or new first-time parents are examples of adults motivated to learn how to deal with their new social roles. They will naturally be among the most responsive to a class on marriage or parenting. The same is true of any adult undergoing the stress and demands of life's transitions.

Adults Have Different Learning Motives

Research has identified three types of adult learners.[7] The first is *goal-oriented learners*. These people use learning to gain specific, concrete objectives. For example, they may be intent on learning to speak in public, or to deal with a particular family problem, or to use better business practices. They will select whatever method that best achieves their purpose—taking a course, joining a group, reading a book, or taking a trip. This need-to-know motivation is basically an extrinsic reward for learning. Most adult learners fall within this group. They learn only to reach a goal; it is a means to an end, not the end itself.

The second type of adult learner is *activity-oriented learners*, who participate primarily for the sake of the activity itself rather than to develop a skill or to learn a subject matter. They may take a course or join a group to escape loneliness, boredom, an unhappy home, or even to find a spouse. This is unrelated to a reward for learning, but is related to the activity involved—meeting new people, getting out of the house, etc.

Learning-oriented learners make up the third group. They pursue learning for its own sake. They simply enjoy learning, and desire to know and to grow through learning. Most are avid readers and enjoy watching serious television programs. These are the people who make extensive background preparations when traveling in order to appreciate what they see. This "learning-is-its-own-reward" approach is basically intrinsic. Learning is not a means to an end, it *is* the end.

Keep in mind that all three types of adult learners are involved in adult educational ministries. Some come to Sunday school to find answers to their life problems. Others come primarily because of habit, they enjoy going to class and enjoy the fellowship they find there. Still others come because they enjoy learning about the Bible, and they want to know more just for the sheer joy of learning. We must also recognize that many adults come with a mix of these motivations.

The Stages and Transitions of Adulthood 3

W hat is your life? You are a mist that appears for a little while and then vanishes" (James 4:14). For those with no hope of resurrection this is a depressing thought. In fact some use the brevity of life as a reason to "eat, drink, and be merry."

However, the shortness of life can motivate the believer to use time wisely. The Psalmist prayed, "Teach us to number our days aright, that we may gain a heart of wisdom" (Psalms 90:12). There is a wisdom that comes from "numbering our days," from looking at the process of life and what each phases is meant to accomplish in God's plan. This chapter looks at the stages of adulthood, and how they apply to Christian education ministries.

CHANGE — THE ONLY CONSTANT

From the initial union of two parental cells in the womb we are changing. Through constant cell replacement our bodies are completely replaced about every 7 years. Change is not limited to the physical, however. It also involves the mind, the emotions, the spirit, our relationships, and social responsibilities. Change in childhood and adolescence is rapid, dramatic, and easily observed. In comparison, adulthood appears relatively stable, but it is not static. Changes continue throughout one's lifetime.

Change is the key word in adulthood. As Charles Sell puts it, "Life goes on—from one thing to the next, one crisis to another.

Life may better be described by prepositions than by nouns. Life seems to be en route: to, from, into, out of, through. Fixed points are few, transitions many. Life is made up of passages. The glory does not lie in arriving; it lies in getting there."[8]

Teachers can be agents of change, helping adults cope with life's changes and helping them discover God's will for life. "Be transformed by the renewing of your mind. Then you will be able to test and approve what God's will is" (Romans 12:2).

Of course, not all changes are good. Nevertheless, the believer can be comforted in that even in the midst of change God maintains the power to move us toward His will for us. "We know that in all things God works for the good of those who love him, who have been called according to his purpose." (Romans 8:28,29).

God wants life's transitions to be times of growth and fulfillment. The more we, as teachers, understand the transitions of adulthood and the dynamics at work within them, the more effectively we can guide adults to appropriate learning.

For decades educators and psychologists have scrutinized the development of infants, toddlers, and adolescents. Not until recently has serious attention been given to the developmental phases, needs, and characteristics of adults. Many of the changes occur in predictable patterns of physical, psychological, social, and even spiritual development. We need to recognize that, like childhood, adulthood is also a developmental period.

DEVELOPMENT OF SOCIAL ROLES AND TASKS

Unlike other creatures, human beings are not born with an instinct that programs us to make our way successfully through life. A human being must learn his way through life. This path of learning is lifelong, from cradle to grave. It is not gradual and steady, it is characterized more by occasional spurts and steep climbs, interspersed with plateaus of less change. These crisis periods of learning are known as "developmental tasks."

Robert J. Havighurst defines a developmental task as: "A task which arises at or about a certain period in the life of the individual, successful achievement of which leads to his happi-

Havighurst's Developmental Tasks

Early Adulthood	1. Selecting a mate (or adjusting to unmarried adult status). 2. Learning to live with a marriage partner. 3. Starting a family. 4. Rearing children (or learning to relate to the children of others.) 5. Managing a home. 6. Getting started in an occupation. 7. Taking a civic responsibility. 8. Finding a congenial social group.
Middle Adulthood	1. Achieving adult civic and social responsibility. 2. Establishing and maintaining an economic standard of living. 3. Assisting teenage children to become responsible and happy adults. 4. Developing adult leisure time activities. 5. Relating oneself to one's spouse as a person. 6. Accepting and adjusting to the physiological changes of middle age. 7. Adjusting to aging parents.
Later Maturity	1. Adjusting to decreasing physical strength and health. 2. Adjusting to retirement and reduced income. 3. Adjusting to death of spouse. 4. Establishing an explicit affiliation with one's age group. 5. Meeting social and civic obligations. 6. Establishing satisfactory physical living arrangements.

ness and to success with later tasks, while failure leads to unhappiness in the individual, disapproval by the society, and difficulty with later tasks."[9] Three primary forces lead the individual to accomplish these developmental tasks: physical maturation, cultural pressures of society, and the individual's personal values and aspirations.

Progress through adulthood, using Havighurst's model, can be measured in terms of acquiring the skills needed to complete certain tasks necessary to deal with the physical and social changes of life. For example, learning to select a mate, learning to manage a home, becoming a parent, adjusting to retirement, or accepting the end of one's life. Fulfillment in life is linked to the successful accomplishment of each group of tasks in proper sequence. Failure results in arrested development, personal frustration, and disapproval from society.

Keep in mind that Havighurst's research was based on studies of middle-class Americans in traditional family circumstances. This, of course, fails to reflect the less privileged or the developmental tasks of single adults. Nevertheless, Havighurst's list of developmental tasks are still useful signposts by which to measure progress in adult development.

DEVELOPMENT OF THE ADULT INNER MAN

Just as we are indebted to the insightful observations of Havighurst on social development, we can also benefit from the work of Erik Erikson who focused on what he called ego or self-development, which is the development of inner values. For our purposes, we could say Havighurst looked at a person's relationships with others, while Erikson looked at a person's development within. Erikson did not consider the inner man as an evangelical Christian might use the term, nevertheless his analysis is helpful.

Erikson observed that in each stage of development each individual faces a crisis of tension between two inner values. A person's success in each stage of development depends on how he resolves this tension by his choices and behaviors. When the

EIGHT AGES OF EGO DEVELOPMENT

Age	Tension/Polarity	Virtue From Successful Resolution
EARLY INFANCY (birth to 1 year)	Trust VS. Mistrust	Drive & Hope
LATER INFANCY (1 to 3 years)	Autonomy VS. Shame	Self-control & Will Power
EARLY CHILDHOOD (4 to 6 years)	Initiative VS. Guilt	Direction & Purpose
MIDDLE CHILDHOOD (6 to 11 years)	Industry VS. Inferiority	Method & Competence
ADOLESCENCE (12 to 20 years)	Ego Identity VS. Role Confusion	Devotion & Fidelity
EARLY ADULTHOOD	Intimacy vs. Isolation	Affiliation & Love
MIDDLE ADULTHOOD	Generativity VS. Stagnation	Production & Care
LATE ADULTHOOD	Integrity VS. Despair	Renunciation & Wisdom

resolution is successful a specific virtue emerges that blesses the individual and his world. Like Havighurst, Erikson maintained that success in each stage leads to happiness while failure brings misery.

Early Adulthood - Intimacy vs. Isolation

Erikson's model views the early adult years as a crisis of tension between *intimacy* and *isolation*. The young adult, to be fulfilled and happy in life, needs to move toward the development of intimacy with others. Intimacy is defined as the ability to share oneself with others openly and without fear of ego damage. This is necessary to commit to others in friendship, in marriage, or in any interpersonal relationship. In fact, success in the workplace depends on one's ability to relate to others.

If a young adult does not move toward developing intimacy, he will move toward isolation. He will avoid situations that require learning intimacy skills. The result is isolation from others, a sense of alienation and self-absorption. This failure to relate openly to others, and the resulting self-centeredness, has been noted as a cause behind the widespread abuse of drugs and promiscuity. Both efforts numb the sense of isolation.

Middle Adulthood - Generativity vs. Stagnation

The middle-aged years are a conflict between tendencies toward *generativity* and *stagnation*. Remember, it is our choices and behaviors that force us to move in one direction or the other.

Generativity means being productive in the broadest sense through creative pursuits in career, leisure time activities, child-rearing, teaching, caring, volunteer work, etc. It reflects an interest in helping to establish and to guide the next generation. A person exhibiting this inner value attaches meaning to life after his or her death. It is important to this person to contribute something that will outlive self.

Stagnation refers to preoccupation with one's own importance and being unable to make an investment in the lives of others. This individual tends to be egocentric, nonproductive, and self-indulgent. He may become depressed thinking he cannot contribute to others. Unfortunately, both this individual and those around him are losers. Adults gravitating toward stagnation are ill-prepared to face the closing years of life because they will have to deal with hardened selfishness, and will regret that little or nothing will outlive them.

Late Adulthood - Integrity vs. Despair

The later years of adulthood, according to Erikson, are a conflict in tension between *integrity* and *despair*. Integrity refers to a sense that life has been productive and worthwhile; one has managed to cope with life's triumphs as well as with its disappointments. Despite mistakes and some regrets, this individual is able to look back on life with general satisfaction. Life has been rich and meaningful. The fact that life is coming to a close, that he has spent his one-and-only life cycle, is accepted gracefully. Death is viewed as a natural event in his total life journey.

Despair characterizes the individual who has not successfully negotiated the stages of adult life. His choices and behaviors have brought him a sense of hopelessness and feelings of self-disgust. He is bitter over past failures. He anguishes in feelings of a wasted life. Valuable time has slipped away and not enough has been accomplished. There is despair that he won't have another chance. Death is feared, in this case, because it eliminates forever all possibility of correcting past mistakes. These people die unhappy and unfulfilled.

TRANSITION TIMES IN THE ADULT LIFE

The most critical time an adult faces seems to be when he is making the transition from one stage of life to another. These transition points also include those times when a person's normal life-style is disrupted by events that produce pain, discomfort, crisis, or change. Specific events that often initiate these changes in our roles, relationships, routines and assumptions are called "marker events" since they mark a transition from one phase of life to another.

Some transitions are normally expected and bring relatively

little stress. These include getting married, becoming a parent, starting a new job, or retiring. Other transitions are unanticipated and often disruptive, such as major surgery, a car accident, being laid off work, a divorce, or the death of one's spouse. Understandably, these unanticipated transitions are unpredictable and more stressful.

People experience the full spectrum of emotions during transitions. Depending on the nature of the crisis, these may include joy, guilt, disappointment, anxiety, apprehension, or loss of self-esteem. People may struggle to keep their emotional, mental, or even spiritual balance; prolonged times of stress may even bring physical illness.

Transitions are crisis times in an adult's life. They may not be catastrophic or dramatic, but they are still a crisis in the sense that these times are *turning points* in life. Again quoting Charles Sell, "Life has moments when we are like a trapeze artist swinging high above the crowd. He stuns the audience by letting go of one bar to seize another. Between the bars, he is precariously afloat in midair. The audience gasps as he dangles on nothing but his fading momentum. His life depends on his ability to grab hold of the bar swinging toward him. Between the letting go and the grabbing on, there is no turning back...transitions are really life's most crucial places, leading to either renewal or ruin."[10]

APPLICATIONS FOR CHRISTIAN EDUCATION

Man is a multidimensional being; he is physical, emotional, mental, spiritual, and social. To which of these is adult Christian education directed? How you answer this question will dictate what kind of teaching you give to the adults in your classroom. The answer is all of them!

We must realize that human beings are a whole; they do not come in components that exist separately. In other words, adults do not lay aside the nonspiritual aspects of their lives when they enter the Sunday school. Whatever is going on in their lives impacts them throughout. The mental, emotional, spiritual, physical and social all overlap. What happens in one affects all the others. Therefore, we need to be concerned and aware of what is happening in all dimensions of a person's life. The more we understand the transitions of adulthood and the dynamics at work within those life-stages, the more effectively we can minister to adults.

From Havighurst's Developmental Tasks

Fundamental to understanding adult learning is their motivation to learn the knowledge and skills needed to solve a problem, to answer a question, or to meet a need. Many of these needs are developmental tasks, tasks arising at a certain time in life which must be mastered to live successfully. The particular developmental task an adult is facing is, to him, his major problem to be solved. It is very important, therefore, for us to be aware of the developmental tasks our students are facing.

We want the adults attending our Sunday school classes to be highly motivated; eager to understand and apply God's Word to their lives. It is only wisdom, therefore, to tap the natural motivation most adults have related to developmental tasks. Malcolm Knowles, a secular specialist in adult education, has stated,

> "Andragogy [helping adults learn] assumes that learners are ready to learn those things they 'need' to because of the developmental phases they are approaching in their roles as workers, spouses, parents, leisure time users, and the like. The critical implication of this assumption is the importance of timing learning experiences to coincide with the learners' developmental tasks."[11]

If problem-solving is the primary concern of adults, then developmental tasks present us with the primary *schedule* of problems to be solved. With this knowledge, we can prepare appropriate learning opportunities and equip adults for life.

From Erikson's Development of Self and Inner Values

Erikson's observations suggest that young adults need to develop the skills and capacity for intimacy. Christian teachers can help adults understand that only in Christ can one find true acceptance and intimacy, first with God and then with others. Helping young adults walk with Christ enables them to develop the capacity for intimacy, so vital to marriage, to work, and to social relationships.

Middle adults need to be developing an active concern for those around them, becoming productive and caring. Again, Christians understand that such altruistic qualities come from the new life one finds in Christ. God's Word and the work of His Spirit within us produce the caring, self-giving life that contributes to the enrichment of others. As the Apostle Paul said, "For Christ's love compels us.... Those who live should no longer live for themselves but for him who died for them and was raised again" (2 Corinthians 5:14,15). Christian adults, especially in their middle years, should "look not only to [their] own interests, but also to the interests of others" (Philippians 2:4).

Christians would agree with Erikson that the choices and behaviors of one's early- and middle-adult years will have consequences in later adulthood. Whether one ends his life in contentment and peace, or in despair and bitterness will depend on how much of God's truth he or she has incorporated into life. The apostle Paul exemplifies an adult who could look back on life, and forward to eternity with what Erikson called "integrity." He shared such feelings with Timothy, "For I am already being poured out like a drink offering, and the time has come for my departure. I have fought the good fight, I have finished the race, I have kept the faith. Now there is in store for me the crown of righteousness, which the Lord, the righteous Judge, will award to me on that day—and not only to me, but also to all who have longed for his appearing" (2 Timothy 4:6–8).

From Transition Times in Adulthood

Transitions can be times of doubt, frustration, and uncertainty. Most of us would choose to avoid such trials if we could. But as James exhorts us, we should "Consider it pure joy...whenever you face trials of many kinds, because you know that the testing of your faith develops perseverance. Perseverance must finish its work so that you may be mature and complete, not lacking anything" (James 1:2–4). Let's consider some of the hidden blessings of transitions.[12]

■ Transitions strip away false securities and can create a renewed dependency on God.

■ Transitions turn us to the Scriptures to evaluate goals and priorities.

■ Transitions can be times of starting over and refreshing stagnated routines.

■ Transitions are an exercise in living by faith.

■ Transitions are a time to learn that God is faithful.

We have briefly reviewed some of the dynamics associated with change in the adult years. We have listed some of the developmental tasks adults must master to successfully negotiate the challenges of society. We have seen how the choices and behaviors of adults will develop either positive or negative inner values and conditions. We have also seen that at each turn and in each change adults face a crisis, a turning point in life.

The teaching ministry can have a profound influence on the quality of life for adults. Through it God allows us to share His work of bringing abundant life to His children. Apart from the wisdom and training we receive from God's Word we would be at the mercies of the enemy. As Jesus warned, "The thief comes only to steal and kill and destroy; I have come that they may have life, and have it to the full" (John 10:10).

The Christian teacher can help adults live their faith in a pagan society. The adult years are not only a great adventure, but also a great challenge. There are critical tests that can bring either growth or ruin. May our lives and our teaching ministry comfort adults with the truth that, "No temptation [test, transition, or trial] has seized you except what is common to man. And God is faithful; he will not let you be tempted beyond what you can bear. But when you are tempted, he will also provide a way out so that you can stand up under it" (1 Corinthians 10:13).

Ministry to the Young Adult 4

F or our purposes, we will consider young adults as those
between the ages of 18 to 35. However, the idea that
adulthood begins with high school graduation is being
challenged by those who consider the ages of 18 to 22 to be more
accurately a transition period between adolescence and adulthood. Jerry Stubblefield, in *A Church Ministering to Adults*,
raises this point. "Those from the ages of eighteen to twenty-two
have many of the privileges and advantages of adulthood but do
not usually carry the corresponding responsibilities."[13]

Aside from these considerations, by age 22 to 25 a young man
or woman is considered to be an adult. The young-adult years are
a time of tremendous transition, from dependence on parents to
self-sufficiency, from single life to marriage (for many), from
child to spouse to parent, from student to professor and perhaps
back to student, from church attendee to church leader.

Interpersonal relationships are a primary concern for young
adults. This consists of two parallel themes: identity or individuality (concerning self), and intimacy (concerning others). Success with the former is a prerequisite for success with the latter.
Developing self-identity and intimacy with others is a difficult
business, as evidenced by one author calling the initial period
"Pulling Up Roots" and the remainder of young adulthood "The
Trying Twenties."[14]

Wrestling with one's identity begins in adolescence, but continues into young adulthood. As Gail Sheehy puts it, "Before 18,

the motto is loud and clear: 'I have to get away from my parents.' But the words are seldom connected to action."[15] But after 18, college, military service, and travel provide young adults the chance to flex some independence muscle while still feeling the safety of being connected to family. Young adults attempt to separate themselves from parents and family by latching on to other beliefs that they can call their own.

Establishing independence from parents and a self-identity is handled differently by each individual. We cannot stereotype young adults. For example, the church has traditionally lumped young adults into a group called "College and Career." However, the college student's world is drastically different from life of the career person. His life-style, values, goals and schedules are very different, as are those of the single adult versus the married adult within this age-level. This is important to keep in mind when dealing with young adults in the church.

The search for intimacy addresses the problem of Genesis 2:18, "It is not good for the man to be alone." Too many young adults fail to distinguish between intimacy and sexuality. While "becoming one flesh" is part of intimacy within marriage, intimacy itself is not defined by physical relationships. An adult can be and should be intimate with other adults. Intimacy can be thought of as a quality of relationship in which one can open one's self to another without fear of rejection or being hurt.

Developmentalists stress the importance of intimacy in adult development. The intimacy skills learned in young adulthood impact other adult issues such as marriage, establishing a home, working relationships, and developing long-lasting friendships.

Identity and intimacy are two sides of the same coin; success with one depends on the other. As one writer notes, achieving these in balance is a mark of maturity.

> "This ability to achieve intimacy with another while still maintaining a personal identity and independence is probably the most significant indication of maturity in young adulthood. Possibly this stage of development could properly be called interdependence; the individual retains a personal identity while at the same time entering into a

meaningful relationship with another that calls for giving and even sacrifice if that relationship is to be successful...."[16]

Many young adults suffer from feelings of loneliness. They have severed many adolescent associations in high school and they are also dealing with the harsh reality of life outside the "nest." New relationships may not yet have been formed. The pressures of setting up one's life—job, marriage, home, bills, new friends—are severe. These factors combine to make it very difficult for the individual to feel needed. There are bound to be some feelings of being detached.

The young adult who does not learn the skills of intimacy in relating to other adults will only compound this natural sense of personal isolation. Fear of being rejected or simply not having the self-confidence to open one's self to another will isolate a young adult from social relationships. Sadly, this can hinder the development of related skills and tasks throughout his or her adult years.

DEVELOPMENTAL TASKS

Most of life's major decisions are made during the young adult years, making it perhaps the most exciting and certainly a crucial period of life. While authorities may propose different years to define young adulthood, perhaps nothing better defines it than the developmental tasks listed here. As one person observed, "young adults have only one characteristic in common—they are young at the business of being adults."[17]

An adult's happiness and usefulness later in life correspond to their success at achieving the following tasks of young adulthood:

1. Completing or continuing education.
2. Selecting a mate.
3. Learning to live with a marriage partner.
4. Starting a family.
5. Rearing and developing relationships with children.
6. Managing a home.

7. Getting started in an occupation.
8. Taking on civic responsibility.
9. Finding a congenial social group.

These tasks represent some of the major expectations of society for this age-group. We must understand, of course, that not every young adult will work through all of these in the same way or at the same time. Some older adolescents may already have entered the beginning stages of these tasks, while some middle-adults have not completely worked through all of them. Again, individuality is a major factor for the teacher of young adults to keep in mind.

Completing Or Continuing Education

Most young adults are involved in continuing education. For many it is by entering college or the military, but even entering the work force will require some kind of job training. Each situation will influence the young adult differently, creating subgroups within the general classification of young adult.

For example, consider life on the college campus. The isolation of the campus from the mainstream of adult society will postpone some adult tasks and responsibilities, while creating others. The concern for academic success (or failure) and its impact on dreams of future occupational goals weighs heavily on a college student's mind. The unique and somewhat artificial social context of campus life is another factor that makes the needs, concerns and behavior of a college student different from other young adults. The same could be said for the unique conditions faced in the military.

A Sunday school teacher of young adults should take the time to consider the particular life context of his or her students. Doing so better allows the teacher to understand their needs and best apply lesson truths.

Selecting A Mate

Selecting a mate is one of the most interesting and exciting times of life and yet it is the most disturbing and demanding of all the developmental tasks for this age-level. Since this is to be a lifelong choice, it is vitally important that great care go into the choice. Society may have relaxed its moral standards and encouraged a casual approach to marriage, but God's Word still provides the Christian young adult with a clear message of God's will for his life.

The process includes finding someone who will be the lifelong friend, lover, advisor, and business partner, not to mention one who will meet the social demands of the mate's job or profession. Culture determines the full details, but this selection of a mate is generally the sole responsibility of the young man or woman with little or no interference by parents.

We will consider the single adult in chapter 7. However, it could be noted here that many more young adults are postponing marriage. Toward the latter young-adult years, ages 30 to 35, the developmental task becomes learning to accept singleness. This is not a problem for those who early on decided to remain single, but it can be a very important and difficult task for someone who had always imagined themselves as being married as an adult.

Learning To Live With A Marriage Partner

After the wedding comes the task of learning to live intimately with another human being. This involves learning to communicate and learning to express feelings of love, anger, joy, sorrow, pleasure, and disgust. Through adjustment and self-denial the two must *work* out the commitment that has been made.

Fulfillment and satisfaction from the sexual relationship tend to make the task easier. However, this has been so overstressed in American society that sexual fulfillment is at times the only thing sought, leading to disillusionment.

Some of the tests young married adults face are unexpected pregnancy, financial emergencies, religious differences, illness, divergent personal habits and hobbies, confusion of roles both inside and outside the home, and disagreements over money matters. If both mates are working, the physical stress of working outside the home makes the sharing of household duties imperative. Unhealthy dependence upon parents will also hinder young adults. It is very difficult to fulfill this developmental task if at every crisis one or both mates look to parents for reinforcement, for consolation, or for rescue.

Starting A Family

Having the first child brings profound changes to a marriage. Using birth control techniques available today many couples are postponing having children preferring to first establish careers and financial stability. Once the decision to have children has been made, two-career couples must make decisions about whether or not one spouse will quit his or her job, about child care, about financial adjustments, and more. How these problems are addressed will be greatly influenced by the background of each mate. They may also be the source of conflict and crisis in the marriage. Because of their great concerns with the start of a family, young adults are very receptive to special training courses and counseling offered to help them with this task.

Rearing Children

The responsibilities of rearing children are greater than many young adults comprehend before the child's birth. How will the children be disciplined? What values, beliefs, and ethics should be taught? How are these taught? Parents must understand child development and be prepared to guide and direct children to help them succeed. Again, the great sense of inadequacy young couples may feel about parenting is a prime motivation for them to seek help. Churches that offer classes on parenting will be attractive to young married adults.

Managing A Home

Living on one's own is a major sign of adulthood for most young adults. One of the consequences of young adults postponing marriage is a corresponding delay in moving out of the parent's home. This trend has been well-noted, and seems to be unrelated to the young adult's financial status.

Establishing a home is exciting, but routine and mundane chores must also be done. The home must be kept clean, furniture purchased, repairs made, and meals prepared. Each of these takes money and time. Although cultural expectations have changed some in recent years, the male is still considered the primary provider, and he follows a scriptural pattern when he fulfills this task.

The woman, if she does not work outside the home, must adjust to his income and learn to manage the home within its limits. Unemployment or employment below a couple's original expectations can bring tension into the home. If the wife works, as is more frequently the case, the couple may have an adequate income to cover expenses, but they must learn to adjust to the time and work commitments of both jobs, as well as to each other's fatigue at day's end.

Training on budgeting and financial planning is appropriate for young adults. While the church must be involved in this task, the couple will need to work out the details for their particular situation. Home and budget management will directly affect the social activities that the couple can or cannot participate in. Any entertainment, either inside or outside the home, will be determined by the overall management of the home.

Getting Started In An Occupation

Getting started in an occupation is a major task for young adults. While many people have made preliminary career decisions in late adolescence as part of their education plans, some young adults may still be uncertain about an occupation or career even after college or military experience. A person's self-image and his sense of purpose are intermeshed with occupation and career. This is an extremely important time, and young adults must be encouraged to keep God in the picture. Seeking God should be a part of the overall guidance system provided in Christian education. The church may even consider assisting its young adults in the area of vocational guidance.

Taking On Civic Responsibility

Assuming civic responsibility can involve participation in civic orders, political organizations, service groups, or the church.

Many young adults are extremely concerned with their community and its problems; others may become preoccupied with managing a home, raising children, and getting settled in an occupation and will delay taking on civic responsibility. The financial situation of the couple may also affect their acceptance of civic responsibility. As finances increase, so will social involvement. The church must help young adults understand how they can play an important part in the civic affairs of their society while influencing society as representatives of God's kingdom.

Finding A Congenial Social Group

Loneliness is a reality for young adults. It is more than a lack of social activity; it is symptomatic of our human condition. This is what drives many young singles to flock to bars; they are wanting to relieve their emptiness. Some young adults mistakenly think marriage is the cure for this loneliness. The church must lead young adults to understand loneliness to be "an indication of our incompleteness—of our brokenness...to come to terms with our incompleteness is to understand the confession necessary for ultimate healing."[18] The church must present a personal relationship with Christ as the best and only real solution to the human problem of loneliness.

Terry Hershey, in his book *Young Adult Ministry*, sees a mistake in viewing "ministry with young adults as programs which are designed to take away loneliness. Such a philosophy only increases our busyness. We advertise that we exist 'to take people's loneliness away.' The result? Incessant activity; increased hype; and a fear of silence, thinking and dialogue."[19] What young adults need, says Hershey, is a sense of belonging, a sense of community.

> The issue is our need to take away people's loneliness by keeping them busy. Ministry begins by acknowledging our loneliness and recognizing that community is a place where we can be real—and where we can belong. How do we respond to this pressure of loneliness? The answer is graphically pictured in a theme song, 'You wanna be where everybody knows your name.' We need to belong.[20]

Yet, another aspect of loneliness *is* a lack of social activity. While social activity is not a cure for the deeper loneliness referred to above, it is still a basic human need. Keep in mind that both leaving high school or college and getting married will tend to dissolve many relationships. Helping young adults find healthy outlets for this need is one part of young adult ministry.

IMPLICATIONS FOR CHRISTIAN EDUCATION

While the adult is young and searching, there are moments of extreme mental alertness when reason and curiosity come to the forefront. They are keen to new ideas and opinions because of their intellectual searching. There is freedom to explore.

Concerning Christian education, the young adult years contain the greatest of teachable moments and yet too often the barest of teaching efforts in the church. Young adults face many opportunities that bring with them an unusual readiness for learning.

Young adult ministry is vitally important for helping young adults successfully negotiate the developmental tasks of this period. The young adult is establishing his or her own system of values, and will benefit from the support and influence of other young adults in the church setting. The church must become a part of the life of the individual during these years or he will be lost from further service to God.

A high visibility and high quality effort by the Christian education program will build strong young adults and strong churches. The church can reach out to the young adult in a variety of settings: meetings in a local restaurant, single's fellowship retreats, home Bible study or care groups, fellowship activities, and a strong variety of electives relating Christian teaching to the developmental tasks young adults are facing.

The teacher should work to help young adults in developing their relationships with God, themselves, and others. Remember, it is important for them to develop relationships and intimacy, but intimacy with God is the essential foundation for developing intimacy with others.

Ministry to the Middle Adult 5

The middle adult years run from 35 to 65 years of age. Some people, wanting to further clarify the issue, may refer to "younger middle adults" (ages 35 to 50) and "older middle adults" (ages 50 to 64). For our purposes we will include both in the broader scope of middle adult.

Keep in mind that the age classifications we use are not precise. Different authors will define young, middle, and older adults slightly differently. But the age-level needs and the characteristics generally hold true. Of course, specific individuals may or may not match the general observations made about a certain age-group.

Middle adults are probably the least written about, the least studied, and the neediest group of all. These are the leaders of society, they pay the bills, raise the children, solve the problems, and provide leadership in the home, in the church, and in the community. Generally speaking, these are probably the most productive and fruitful years of life.

DEVELOPMENTAL TASKS OF MIDDLE ADULTHOOD

Middle age is a difficult period of life to admit to, yet it is full of potential fulfillment. Persons in this age-group need to achieve the following developmental tasks which are said to be "reciprocal," since the members of the family react with one another.[21]

- Achieving adult civic and social responsibility.
- Establishing and maintaining an economic standard of living.
- Helping teenage children become responsible and happy adults.
- Developing adult leisure-time activities.
- Relating to one's spouse as a person.
- Accepting and adjusting to the physiological changes of middle age.
- Adjusting to aging parents.

Let's take a close look at each of these.

Achieving Adult Civic And Social Responsibility

Tradition and social pressures encourage the middle adult to become actively involved. He is the backbone of American civic and social life. Involvement outside the home, at work, and at church, along with the tasks of making money and seeking professional fulfillment, can produce special pressures and strains on the adult and his family relationships.

The woman can also be very much involved in the civic and social activities of the community. Because the children are reaching an age of self-sufficiency, the woman has more time to explore and involve herself in volunteer activities.

Another factor that allows for greater civic participation in this age-level is life philosophy. The middle adult has established a fairly definite philosophy of life by this time. This helps him to be confident and secure in decisions and activities that would have been threatening to him earlier in his life.

Social life and friendships are still very important to the middle adult even though his circle of friends has grown smaller and activities quieter. The mobility of our population increases the need for leaders to help and to encourage the establishment of friendships among middle adults. In the United States one out of five families moves every year. Thus, there is a frequent shifting of friendships, neighbors, and social responsibilities.

Establishing And Maintaining An Economic Standard Of Living

The middle adult is reaching the peak of his or her earning power. Many financial pressures, however, often more than offset the level of pay increases. Years of high cost of living and inflation can eat away savings and investments. Major expenses such as emergency health costs, education of the children, retirement funding, and children's marriages call for great efforts in budgeting.

Media advertising also encourages the person to "keep up with the Joneses." This pressure can lead to both spouses working or to one spouse working two jobs. The family must successfully face and adjust to each of those circumstances to maintain good family relationships.

Closely related to this area are the middle adults' feelings about his vocational success or the lack thereof. Middle adults usually enjoy a sense of satisfaction and progress as vocational plans are achieved. However, the opposite may also be true. A great deal of frustration and feelings of failure may exist if vocational goals remain unrealized.

Helping Teenage Children Become Responsible And Happy Adults

Three main individuals are involved at this time of life: the male adult, the female adult, and the child. Each plays several roles. The male is seen as a man, a husband, the household provider, and a father. The female is seen as a woman, a mother, a family and home manager, and a wife. The child is viewed as a person and a member of the household. These interpersonal relationships are delicate and key to proper fulfillment of the various household tasks.

The importance of parental guidance cannot be over-stressed. This task must begin much earlier in the child's life if it is to be truly successful, but the finishing touches are made during the teen years. Emotional maturity is at the depths of this task. The parent must learn to release the child, and the child must learn to become independent while still maintaining the proper attitude toward his parents.

The guidance that the parents give their teens will not necessarily be the same as they received while they were struggling for independence. Good communication between the parents and their children is extremely important at this time. It will build on the relationship they had during the child's earlier years, and it will greatly affect their future relationship.

Developing Adult Leisure-Time Activities

The changing work habits of American business have given the adult a great amount of free time. There must be time off or the person will destroy himself and his family. This can either be a time of great enjoyment and fulfillment for the person and his family, or it can become a source of boredom and loss.

Civic and social demands can fill a portion of this time, but the individual must be creative in his use of time. This time-management should include enjoyable activities for leisure. The leisure activities of young adulthood will change as will habits and interests. The important thing is for the middle adult to keep learning.

Many public school systems and colleges offer short-term, low-cost continuing education opportunities for adults. An almost infinite variety of topics is offered. A recent offering of classes in one community included oil painting, photography, beekeeping, metal smithing, understanding computers, investing in the stock market, candy making, wallpapering, auto mechanics, effective oral communication, floral design, and hundreds of other topics in history, crafts, medicine, music, travel, and business. These courses can bring enrichment and excitement, as well as help keep adults informed.

Relating Oneself To One's Spouse

Among the primary needs of the middle adult is the need for affection. The end of young adulthood and the beginning of the middle adult years presents many critical stresses in the marriage relationship. In fact, nearly 60 percent of divorces occur between 25 and 39 years of age.[22] The number of divorces, then, is directly related to the type of relationship that was developed in the early years of marriage.

With the children gone or reaching an age of independence, the husband and wife face a new situation. When the children demanded a great deal of attention, the husband and wife may have grown apart without realizing this was happening. Now is the time for renewing interpersonal relationships.

An interesting role reversal has been noted concerning the marriage relationship. Early in marriage the wife is usually the one wanting to develop intimacy and a stronger relationship, her orientation is inward. The husband's orientation is outward; his preoccupation is with his career. During the later middle adult years, however, the man, with career goals reached or abandoned, may turn his attention back into the relationship. Now he is the one wanting intimacy and time together. The woman, on the other hand, is now released from the duties of child rearing to develop an identity outside the home.

Now is the time for the couple to begin "dating" one another again. Courtesy and appreciation toward the spouse need to be reinforced.

This increased time together can deepen love and strengthen communication. The husband may need encouragement and understanding while adjusting to changes in his job. The wife will need special understanding while going through the psychological and physiological changes of menopause. The relationship that matures during this period of stress and change will be exceptionally strong when facing the older years.

Accepting And Adjusting To The Physiological Changes Of Middle Age

Many biological changes related to aging are evidenced during the middle adult years. These have been characterized by many humorous statements about the physiology of the middle adult. For example, "You know your over forty when everything hurts and what doesn't hurt doesn't work." Or, "You know your over forty when your knees buckle and your belt won't."

Along with such woes are receding hairlines for men, loss of girlish figures for women, bifocals, and the startling realization that your children are approaching middle age. These are characteristics of the changing adult body.

The individual and the couple must adjust to these changes. There is strong cultural pressure to hide the declining stamina, strength, and energy levels. In fact, the older middle-adult is sometimes unwilling to admit this and will press himself unwisely to prove himself.

The gradual decrease in sexual drive and menopause will affect the couple's relationship. Adjusting to these changes may be difficult. Understanding is needed by all. Most of all, the mirage of youthfulness must be seen for what it really is.

Adjusting to these physical changes will greatly affect one's entire outlook on life. Acceptance can reap many benefits, while failure will result in pain and distortion in other relationships.

Adjusting To Aging Parents

Our society is considered by many to be the most negligent in history concerning the elderly. This attitude carries over into the relationship with aging parents. The term three-generation family comes into clear view. Middle adults are responsible not only for themselves, but for their children and parents. This can be a big drain on an already tight budget.

The older parent looks to the child for support financially, morally, physically, and socially. The death of one parent will greatly increase the other parent's need for companionship. While the children may be moving from the home, the older adult may become a member. A great amount of understanding will be needed. There may be conflicts over headship and authority, and over the budget and expenditures.

To help meet these needs, the church must provide individualized counseling, rather than a formalized learning situation. There is again the tie-in to early childhood relationship development. The communication will be directly proportionate to the quality of the earlier relationships.

IMPLICATIONS FOR CHRISTIAN EDUCATION

The term *mid-life crisis* is a familiar one. Although sometimes over used, it does remind us of a significant truth. The middle adult years are ones of testing and evaluation. Middle adults are testing the values with which they entered adulthood. Values regarding job, family, friends, spiritual life, and even the meaning of success are being scrutinized. They are reevaluating who they are, what they have done compared with what they wanted to do, and whether or not they are accomplishing what is important to them.

The Christian teacher of middle adults needs to be aware of these dynamics in the life of his students. With all the changes taking place, perhaps even disillusionment and a sense of disorientation, the teacher must be prepared to guide middle adults to appreciate and depend upon the unchanging truths of God's Word.

The needs are acute before they come to the surface, so education must take advantage of the teachable moments of crisis and change to articulate the power of God's love. The curriculum of the Sunday school should include opportunities for elective studies as well as for the progressive through-the-Bible studies. Electives should be designed to help middle adults address their developmental tasks during the middle years.

The need is not to retell the Bible stories that they are most likely familiar with, but to help the adult apply Bible truth to life. The teacher's challenge is to present the Bible in a way that is relevant to the middle adult life-stage.

There is a great need for involvement by adult students, not only for effective learning, but also to encourage the development of relationships among the class members. The increase of leisure time will require the use of creative and group approaches to the ministry to the middle-aged person.

Ministry to the Older Adult 6

Older adults, 65 years of age or older, experience a whole new phase of life. It is being a grandparent and having fun with the grandchildren. It is hobbies, memories, fulfillment, and free time. Retirement and changing health induce a retrospective look back as well as a look forward to what the future may hold. There will be adjustment to the death of a mate, which can be very traumatic after many years of living with one person. This is, however, one of the greatest times to enjoy life and the freedoms brought by retirement.

The lack of activity and relaxed living may induce mental laziness. It is important that the older adult continues to see himself as a learner. The latter years of life, even its crises, bring opportunities for learning and development. The older adult should seize all of life and live it to the fullest, but this requires he have a proper outlook. The saying "You are only as old as you think you are" is very important. While there will be declining physical strength, the older adult can remain active if a positive attitude is adopted and activities are chosen wisely.

The retired adult finally has the extra time he longed for during his employment years. Senior adult ministries can use this time to offer opportunities for spiritual fulfillment not possible earlier in life—an overcrowded schedule is no longer a problem. He can devote time to spiritual growth, to increasing his self-worth, and to building up the body of Christ.

DEVELOPMENTAL TASKS OF THE OLDER ADULT

The developmental tasks of older adults center around adjusting to social, physical, mental, and economic limitations—but there are no spiritual limitations. This can help maintain a balanced attitude as the adult recognizes his capabilities.

Havighurst lists the following older adult developmental tasks.[23] Anticipation of new experiences is vital for the successful fulfillment of these tasks:

- Adjusting to decreasing physical strength and health
- Adjusting to retirement and reduced income
- Establishing an explicit affiliation with one's age-group
- Adjusting to death of spouse
- Meeting social and civic obligations
- Establishing satisfactory physical living arrangements

Adjusting To Decreasing Physical Strength And Health

The writer of Ecclesiastes 12:1–8 offers a very poetic description of aging, alluding to the dulling of the senses, the decrease in speed, and the weakening of the body. The older adult years can be a period of significant decline with the threat of illness and disability. Circulation and joint functions are areas most often affected. Arthritis and rheumatism are crippling inflammations in the joint structure. Cardiovascular ailments are common, and vision and hearing also become impaired.

All of these maladies combined can cause the older adult to feel useless. The physiological can and does greatly affect the psychological. The importance of keeping the proper attitude during these years cannot be overstressed. They can either be years of decline or years of beginning, depending on the mental outlook of the individual.

We should not think all older adults are physically debilitated, however. People today are living longer and healthier. The vast majority of older adults enjoy good health and are reasonably active; only a small percentage require intensive care. Nevertheless, it is important that the older adult adjust to the realities of aging and the inevitability of death.

Adjustment To Retirement And Reduced Income

The psychological adjustment to retirement can be significant. For many adults, one's job is the center of existence. When the occupation goes the individual may feel he is of no worth and that he does not count. Work serves to infuse an individual with meaning and self-esteem. It is an important factor in establishing an identity within a given social and economic structure.

A major task connected with retirement is learning to live on a reduced income. There are restrictions on Social Security, and the individual's income is limited. With less income will come less buying power and the need for a tightly controlled budget. These factors combined with inflation may mean the older adult will not have enough funds to support his accustomed life-style.

Financial pressures also come from a new trend. Adults increasingly are reaching older adulthood with their parents still living. In the future, many more retired adults may have either a parent or an older close relative still living for whose care they are at least partially responsible. This will bring an economic impact on both older adults, the nation, and the churches.

Another factor related to retirement is adjusting to more leisure time. The way the individual reacts to this increase in free time has a great deal to do with how he views himself and his later years. There are some who expand hobbies and even make these a source of income. Some take on part-time jobs to assist in the adjustment. The church can provide activities and jobs to tap the resource of older adults.

Adjusting To The Death Of The Spouse

Life expectancy is now approximately 70 years for men and 78 years for women. It has been estimated that over half of the people who have ever lived past 65 years are alive today. Yet with all the health improvements of recent years, eventually the death of a mate will bring the need for adjustment. This is a difficult task, for living with a person for many years brings about dependency and much trust. The loss of the stability of the mate will be traumatic and require adjustment.

There are said to be twice as many widows as widowers in America. Statistics tell us that the average widowed woman will face 20 years of widowhood unless she remarries.

The death of a spouse will mean moving into a smaller house, learning to live without the spouses companionship, learning to prepare meals for one, and handling business affairs and money. All or most of these will be new learning experiences, depending on the background of the individual.

In this situation, the biggest problem will be loneliness. There are problems with moving into the children's home. Since there will probably be grandchildren there may be no extra space. It can be emotionally upsetting to move out of familiar surroundings. The older adult struggles to keep clear communication established with any individual. Declining strength affects communication because a need exists for visual contact and companionship, the things the telephone cannot provide.

Establishing An Explicit Affiliation With One's Age-Group

Senior adults are aware that many of their friends have died, leaving them more alone than they would like to be. They are conscious that younger people have taken their places in work and church. Attitudes of, "I'm not important," "I'm over the hill," and "I'm not needed," may begin to overshadow their thinking.

Facing one's position in life as an older adult is important. The older adult must be able to admit that he or she has reached another level of maturity without seeing it as a death certificate. Life is not over, nor is one's usefulness and capacity to enjoy life.

That is rather harsh and yet it is very true. The older adult must accept his status as a member of the older portion of society. Physiologically, aging slows one down, but this is not necessarily true psychologically. A certain feeling of accomplishment comes with age. The older adult's background is a rich resource. They can share many cherished memories and much hard-learned wisdom with younger generations.

However, this potential is sometimes not valued by others nor tapped for the benefit of the church and family. This leaves older adults struggling to maintain their middle-age companionships that made them feel appreciated. But trying to keep up those relationships and activities becomes increasingly difficult due to the mental and physical changes.

The American society has long been one that worships youth. This causes some older adults to deny a realistic assessment of their state in life. This is a psychological hurdle to jump. They may consider someone their same age to be an older adult, but not themselves. Teaching the middle-aged adult how to cope with approaching retirement is one way to help. This would include a look at the six developmental tasks and options for accepting his position.

Meeting Social And Civic Obligations

The older adult is a growing commercial and political force within society. As the Baby Boom generation grows older, this will continue to be the case; and with medical and nutritional advances, the average life span continues to increase.

The older adult's ability to provide effective leadership depends on his keeping up with the current trends and research in all fields. The older adult must still see himself as productive and as a learner. He should also recognize his years of experience as a rich resource that can benefit others. The temptation to live in the past must be overcome. Development comes only as the person grows. The older adult has tremendous potential, with leisure time as a great advantage.

Establishing Satisfactory Physical Living Arrangements

With the decline of physical strength and the handicaps of illness (such as heart disease and rheumatism), an older adult becomes increasingly aware of his surroundings. He has a need for peace, quiet, and privacy, and also has a need to be close to relatives, to shopping areas, to transportation, and to his social group.

Only 3 to 6 percent of the older adult population lives in

nursing homes. This leaves a vast majority outside such a setting, which requires personal independence of action on his part. The older adult should look for a comfortable, warm, and private setting. This will require planning that should be done during the latter middle years. This will help ensure fulfillment.

IMPLICATIONS FOR CHRISTIAN EDUCATION

A shift is needed in our approach to the education of older adults. The older adult is still able to learn, but he may have greater difficulty remembering. The teacher must recognize that the older adult's reaction time has decreased. Often in a classroom situation his inability to turn pages and hear directions causes him to remain passive. Unfortunately, that is sometimes misinterpreted as a disinterest in learning.

The church must take a second look at the options it offers older adults. They need fellowship with persons of their own age and opportunities for worship, in-depth Bible study, and service. The older adults' occupational, educational, and spiritual years of experience should be put to good use.

The spiritual maturity of age is important. Many older adults have earned the reputations of being the pillars of the church. Their ability to pray, their experience in walking with the Lord, and their habit of faithful attendance at church provides an example and challenge to the rest of the church.

If the adult Sunday school program provides the older adult with opportunities to develop new relationships, to develop new interests and hobbies, and to contribute to the work of the church, this time of life can be the most fruitful for people.

Ministry to the Single Adult

7

Churches that do not learn to incorporate single adults into the life of their church will become increasingly out of touch with the communities they are trying to reach. Consider the facts: nearly 40 percent of the U.S. adult population is single, up from 27 percent in 1965. In some metropolitan areas the percentage is much higher.

The single adult population has grown in part because adults are postponing marriage; the median age for first time marriage is higher today for both men and women than it has been in 90 years. Other contributing factors include the high rate of divorce and the increasingly common choice not to marry. Between 1970 and 1988, the number of single parents with children under 18 in the home more than doubled from 3.8 million to 9.4 million. Single-parent families, as a portion of all family groups with children, increased from 13 percent in 1970 to 27 percent in 1988. "This increase is one of the most important recent changes in family composition, with major implications for poverty and social welfare programs."[24] The church's adult ministries programs must address these realities.

NEEDS OF THE SINGLE ADULT

Single adults have many of the same needs as married adults. One difference, of course, is that the single adult must face their challenges alone or seek help from other adults. We must be careful not to equate singleness with problems. Not all single adults have problems with being single. Many are well-adjusted and happy. Others do have concerns. Unfortunately, many singles feel uncomfortable with the marriage-family bias of the church. Their needs go untreated and their potential contribution to the body of Christ unrealized. Following is a brief review of some needs, issues and concerns of single adults.

To Develop Interpersonal Relationships

All singles need to develop relationships with the opposite sex, both in dating situations and in simple friendships. Meaningful relationships are essential for a meaningful life. Sharing joys and sorrows, discoveries, victories, and defeats are all part of the human experience.

Single adults must be able to converse with adults of the opposite sex without eyebrows being raised. Such conversation and social interaction are an important part of personal development, especially for the young adult. They are also important for successful group dynamics—having the freedom to express oneself without any overtones being read into the setting. The single adult must be free to talk in openness and honesty.

To Integrate Into The Body Of Christ

Spiritually and scripturally, singles are members of the body of Christ. In practice, however, many singles view themselves as on the fringe or on the outside looking in because the strong marriage and family orientation of some churches neglects singles. They feel left out, ignored, or worse, rejected. They are sometimes misunderstood or even mistrusted by married people.

As with any adult, singles need to maintain and develop their spiritual man. All singles need to learn how to pray, how to study the Bible, how to identify their spiritual gifts, and how to pursue outlets of Christian service in order to develop their spiritual life.

To Develop A Single Identity

Each single adult needs to accept and function within his or her singleness. This is not the same as resignation to singleness, for marriage may come in the future. Rather, it is learning to be content and fulfilled in life as a single person. This may include dealing with emotional problems resulting from shattered dreams of marriage, low self-esteem, rejection, loss through death or divorce, sexual sin, and not having a sense of belonging.

Developing a single identity is a more difficult task for singles obsessed with marriage. These singles may succumb to what has been called the "mystique of marriage," the idea that somehow life is better or easier after marriage. For this reason, they may put off or postpone significant decisions until after marriage. These singles feel (even if they do not believe) that once they get married "everything will be good."

To Be Thought Of As A Complete Person

Married adults sometimes view singles as incomplete; as though they are somehow less than what they would be if they were married. The single adult is a complete individual and should not be judged in terms of marital status, that is, never married, divorced, or widowed.

Single adults want to be seen as whole people, not incomplete people desperately searching for their other half. The young single adult is still in the identity-crisis phase of life. Since one's identity partly depends on acceptance by others, it is important that the church's acceptance of single adults be sincere. Viewing the single adult as a whole and complete person leads to expressions of acceptance, which in turn helps the single adult develop an attitude of self-worth.

To Be In Fellowship With Families

The single adult needs family ties. He needs to hear a child laugh or cry. He needs to see love displayed in the family context, and to receive an affectionate child's hug. He needs to witness a healthy marriage relationship between a husband and wife, and to have friends who are married. Some of these needs are met only by being associated with families.

The family can also grow in this association. It will enable children to identify with a Christian adult other than their parents, and see how life can be fulfilling even if God calls one to remain single.

To Socialize With Other Singles

People with similar needs and interests naturally group together. This is a positive thing and should not be feared as being cliquish or antisocial. Single adults are no exception. They need a comfortable setting in which to share interests, concerns, and dreams with others who share their common experience. The church needs to provide a spiritually healthy alternative to the worldly orientation of singles bars. We should also appreciate that a great deal of maturity is developed within the context of such interpersonal relationships and social activities.

To Work Through The Crisis Recovery Process

This refers primarily to the crises of divorce or the death of a spouse. Each brings a significant emotional and spiritual impact. While the process of grief recovery is well defined, the church must not neglect to provide the appropriate programs to assist divorced and widowed adults through that process. Recovery from divorce and widowhood goes beyond the emotional loss of a loved one and the end of a relationship; other matters to consider are disruption to the family, visitation rights, reentry into the workforce, accepting one's new identity as a single adult, mastering money matters and business affairs, and more.

To Assume The Role Of Single Parent

For many single adults the responsibilities and difficulties of parenthood are overwhelming. Men and women do not usually plan on becoming a single parent. But divorce, widowhood, and marital separation force such a life-style on thousands every year, bringing with them feelings that interfere with parenting.

Any church that wants to help single adults must be prepared to help single parents. Provide classes that offer help, and as a teacher make yourself available to the single parent. Listen to their concerns. How do they feel about the church, or their child's Sunday school experience? How can you help them with their parenting problems?

Recognize that many single parents have difficulty becoming involved in a church. For example, if your church has a strong marriage and couple orientation, single parents may feel they are unwelcome or just don't fit in. Financial and childcare constraints also make it difficult for a single parent to participate in the various church activities. A church or Sunday school class should ask, "What can we do to better minister to the needs of our single-parent adults?"

SCRIPTURE AND THE SINGLE LIFE-STYLE

Far from being a demographic oddity, remaining single throughout much or all of one's adult years is a respected lifestyle from a scriptural point of view. In Matthew 19, Jesus' discussion with the Pharisees about marriage and divorce includes these words. "Only those people who have been given the gift of staying single can accept this teaching...Some people stay single for the sake of the kingdom of heaven. Anyone who can accept this teaching should do so" (Matthew 19:11,12, Contemporary English Version).

In 1 Corinthians 7, Paul gives specific instructions to the church and to individuals within the church. His is not a low view of marriage; rather, he is articulating the necessity of self-hood or individuality. He says in verse 7, "Every man hath his proper gift of God, one after this manner, and another after that" (KJV). The context leads us to understand that there are special relationships in life given for a particular type and style of ministry. The single adult, as a rule, has greater potential for developing his Christian service. As his spiritual gifts are recognized by the church, he can apply himself to using his gifts for God's glory. This thought is discussed further in verses 17–24. Paul shows the single or married person that God accepts and values him as he is. The church should do likewise.

The church should be ready to make demands on the singles because they need to see themselves as contributing members of the body of Christ. Paul highlights a principle that will greatly aid the church's approach with the single. "Just as each of us has one body with many members, and these members do not all have the same function, so in Christ we who are many form one body, and each member belongs to all the others. We have different gifts, according to the grace given us" (Romans 12:4–6). First Corinthians 7:32–35 also notes that the relatively unencumbered lifestyle of singles makes them excellent candidates for leadership and service roles.

The single adult is part of the Body, which would be incomplete without this part. Single adults can make a valuable contribution. They should have opportunities of service related to their spiritual gifts. Their Christian service will lead to a stronger and healthier self-image, which in turn, will lead to deeper and more lasting relationships.

IMPLICATIONS FOR CHRISTIAN EDUCATION

The question is, "What is the Sunday school to do about single adults?" Certainly, we cannot afford to ignore or overlook 40 percent of American adults.

Become aware of single adults

Single adults are sometimes overlooked. Conduct a survey within your class, church, and community to discover the number and kinds of singles you can reach. How many always-single adults do you find, how many divorced, how many widowed, how many single parents? Churches often discover many more single adults within their ministry reach than they expected.

Provide an atmosphere of genuine acceptance

The most important thing a teacher can do for singles is to accept them. Keep in mind that ministry with single adults is not meant to promote singleness, nor to promote marriage. We accept adults into the church family as they are. Don't project a when-are-you-going-to-get-married attitude.

Your attitude toward the divorced is also important. Although we strongly oppose divorce, we should not close our eyes to the many people in society who suffer from loneliness, guilt, fear and frustration because of divorce. In Christ's name we minister to all—"whosoever will may come." Offering a divorce-recovery class is one way to help.

Provide for fellowship needs

Single adults are very concerned about their social life. They want and need significant relationships in their lives. Your Sunday school class can provide the small-group identification and support they need.

When planning social activities for adults, especially in classes with both single and married students, don't be so couple oriented that single adults feel uncomfortable or unwelcome. Remember that social interaction between the sexes is normal and healthy, for the single and married alike.

However, keep in mind that a church will likely have singles who are still recovering from the trauma of broken relationships, divorce, or the death of a spouse. They may have returned to the church for just such needs. They may need social activities as part of their recovery, but they need the church to be an emotionally safe place to come for healing. Don't promote social activities as dating events, and by all means reject the idea of singles ministry as a Christian dating service.

Grouping Singles in the Sunday School

Should single adults be given their own class or should they be mixed with married adults? This is a question every Sunday school leadership team must face. There are no simple answers. You must look at your program's goals, the facilities available, and the preferences of the single adults you are trying to reach.

The singles-only classes can best address the problems, interests, and concerns important to single adults, such as loneliness, dating, single parenting, divorce recovery and others. Yet this is not the choice of all single adults. An older never-married single, for example, may struggle with an "I'm-not-married-so-I'm-a-failure" complex. This person may resist acknowledging their singleness by refusing to attend a singles-only class. Another single adult, formerly married for many years and perhaps a parent, may appreciate the freedom to choose between married, single, or mixed-status classes. Forcing them into their own class has other problems also. Such classes may isolate singles from the mainstream of church life, and may make them feel the church wants to insulate itself from interaction with them.

There are benefits to both singles-only and mixed marital status classes, so you may consider periodically varying class groupings. Occassionally offering electives is one way to accomplish this. This keeps groups (single and married) from stagnating or becoming too cliquish. The bottom line is that single adults are *adults*. They appreciate making decisions for themselves, so give them options.

Provide opportunities for service

Provide single adults opportunities for service. As the apostle Paul noted, the somewhat unencumbered life-style of singles makes them excellent candidates for leadership and service roles (1 Corinthians 7:32–35).

Plan to employ your regular single attenders in the work of the class. Appoint them to prepare tables, chairs, song books, papers, etc. Appoint someone to take attendance. Other class members can be responsible for refreshments if you have a fellowship time. Choose hosts and hostesses to welcome everyone upon arrival. Have someone register guests, writing down their telephone number and address and preparing a name tag for them. By the way, it is a good idea for everyone in your class to wear name tags. This not only helps visitors feel at ease but increases the fellowship potential of class time.

A well-planned and smoothly-run class session will help singles feel better about their class. It also will greatly increase the likelihood of visitors returning.

The church must minister to the single adult segment of the adult population. The wise church will recognize single adults as vital members of Christ's body who are reaching out to grow in God. The wise teacher will recognize that the single's time, energy, emotions, and talents can be channeled for God's glory.

Organizing Adults for Learning 8

T he success of the adult Sunday school program depends on many things. One that is given little thought, or sometimes completely overlooked, is how adults are organized for learning. How can adults be grouped to take maximum advantage of their motivation and the church's resources? In *The Christian Education of Adults*, Gilbert Peterson makes the following observation, "Churches usually pay considerable attention to ministries for children and youth. Their programs are well structured, and all types of programs are provided. The same careful planning and attention to detail need to be given to adult programs....If we are going to be serious about Christian education for adults, then effective planning and organization is necessary."[25]

Some feel a church of small size or a class with a good teacher make divisions within an adult Sunday school unnecessary. While a church might function with one adult class, the real issue is whether this is the most effective arrangement.

CONSIDERATIONS ON GROUPING DECISIONS

Facilities

While there are advantages in offering adults a variety of classes to choose from, your facilities will usually determine the number of classes or divisions you can have in your adult program. This is generally beyond the control of most Sunday school teachers.

If your facilities are too limited to provide that variety, explore some creative solutions. Some adult classes could meet at locations nearby the church. Local restaurants or motels may have meeting rooms that the church could rent. A church member may volunteer his home as a workable alternative. Consider getting double use out of your facilities by going to double services. Some Sunday school classes could be offered during an early morning worship service, while another set of classes meet during the second morning service. Consider offering classes during the hour before the evening service, or on a week night. Creativity and flexibility can help solve some facility problems.

Availability Of Teachers

Another consideration related to grouping adults is the availability of teachers. Obviously, offering a growing variety of adult classes requires a growing number of teachers. In most churches there is a shortage of teachers. A forward-looking, growth-oriented church will include an ongoing teacher-training class as part of their adult curriculum. The time for training workers and teachers is *before* they are needed. A quarterly or yearly teacher-training class can supply the church with a pool of prepared workers. As qualified teachers become available new classes can be added and new grouping possibilities explored.

The Demographics of Your Adult Population

The composition of the adults in your church and in the community can provide clues as to the grouping arrangements your adults will find appealing. Generally, adults gravitate toward groups where they find others like themselves. Young adults want to congregate with other young adults. Middle-aged adults find other middle adults, and senior adults enjoy the company of other seniors. This does not mean that age-level groups cannot or should not mix. But it does suggest that a church with sufficient numbers in each of these age-levels should be offering classes and events where adults within an age-level can fellowship together.

Even within age-levels, demographic differences will produce subgroupings. Single adults, newly married couples, parents of teenagers, ethnic groups, career orientations, and many other criteria can be used to define groups. Again, these groups can and should mingle. But they may also appreciate occasional opportunities to meet apart.

Besides these factors, the various developmental stages and life experiences of adult life will also influence an individual's approach to learning and how he will naturally group with others. The more the Sunday school leadership understands the adult composition of their church and the community the more effective they can be in providing groups that attract adults to the church's Christian education ministries.

To summarize:

- Use your facilities and resources for maximum effectiveness. Flexibility and creativity are the keys.
- Be continually training new workers and teachers so new grouping options can be implemented.
- Understand that adults will naturally group themselves with people in common life situations or with common interests.
- Look at other factors that might provide points of commonality to unite adults together for fellowship and learning.
- Never assign adults to a class or dictate who they are to group with. They are self-directed in their approach to educational programs. Treat adults with respect and courtesy.

The grouping alternatives available to a church are virtually limitless. However, some make more educational sense than others; and that, rather than novelty, is our objective. Whichever grouping methods are used, a pupil to teacher ratio of 25 to 1 is generally recommended—that is 1 teacher for every 25 adults. This encourages adults to develop significant friendships in a small-group setting, while allowing the teacher to get acquainted with all of his or her students. A large group hinders some of the small-group benefits, and limits the variety of teaching methods a teacher can use.

Let's look at some of the more widely recognized plans for grouping adults.

GROUPING ADULTS BY AGE

Grouping by age is the most common way of organizing the adult Sunday school. Of course, any attempt to define the age limit of the adult groups is somewhat arbitrary. A small church or one with limiting facilities could group broadly: young adult (18–34), middle adult (35–54), and older adult (55 and over). Some churches have designed classes based on the decade the individual was born in, thus, a class for those born in the 40's, the 50's, the 60's, etc. This arrangement joins adults with common cultural and historic experiences.

Age-grouping offers the individual adult the comfort of knowing that everyone is approximately their own age. Age-grouping will also tend to cluster adults facing similar developmental tasks in life. This sharing of life concerns can make the bond of fellowship all the stronger. To feel as if one belongs and is accepted is important for any lasting participation to occur.

However, age-grouping does not guarantee success. Some people, for example, may feel it is an invasion of their privacy, or a restriction on their autonomy to be arbitrarily grouped by age. They want the freedom to choose their own group.

Age-grouping may also hinder a person's ability to widen his circle of acquaintances to those beyond his own age-group. The purpose of the Sunday school is not to drive people away or to limit them with fixed rules, but to provide a comfortable and conducive atmosphere for learning.

Another difficulty may arise when a married couple's ages place them in two separate age-groupings. The couple may find it difficult to decide with which group to align. When a choice is made, it is important that their choice be honored.

In this whole matter of grouping adults by age, remember

Gilbert Peterson's advice, "In churches where classes are divided by age, there is usually some overlapping of ages and the categories are used for general division rather than rigid classification. Flexibility, tact, and concern for individual needs should be taken into account in any age-graded adult department."[26]

GROUPING ADULTS BY INTEREST OR NEED

Grouping adults by interest or need is accomplished by offering a variety of elective courses within the adult Sunday school program. The individual decides for himself, based on his own interests or perception of need, which topic he will study.

In elective classes adults are grouped together temporarily, perhaps 1 month, 1 quarter, or 1 year depending on the length of the study. But the nature of an elective is that the adult must enroll in the class, and that the class remains together for a specified period of time.

Topics of study could include contemporary social issues, Bible or doctrinal studies, or classes designed to address developmental tasks in the context of the Christian faith, such as money management (stewardship), parenting, marriage enrichment, adjusting to the aging process, and so on. A new convert's class is another example of grouping according to a particular interest or need. The variety of topics is almost limitless. The point to remember is that electives are meant to address adult interests and needs in the context of biblical answers.

Before developing an elective system, the Sunday school leadership needs to consider both the advantages and the disadvantages to the Sunday school and to the adult student.

DISADVANTAGES OF GROUPING BY ELECTIVE

Unbalanced Christian Education
An overemphasis on electives can sidetrack the adult Christian education program from a balanced curriculum. Just as the physical body suffers without a well-rounded diet from all the

important food groups, so spiritual health will suffer if a balanced approach to Bible study and Christian education is neglected. Careful planning can avoid this potential weakness of the elective system. Consider the classes being offered over the course of the quarter and the year. Also consider the long-term by looking at the curriculum balance over 5 and 10 years.

Unbalanced Class Sizes

Electives can lead to unbalanced class size. Some topics and some teachers will naturally draw a larger attendance than others. This may leave some classes too large while others are too small. This can be remedied by limiting the enrollment of such classes. Popular courses can then be repeated quarterly or yearly allowing other adults to benefit from the course.

Disrupted Social Structure

Electives may disrupt existing social structures. It is not unusual for some adults to have been together in the same class for many years. There will be a natural resistance by some to an elective system where class membership changes each quarter.

Husbands and wives may also experience some tension between feeling they must stay with their spouse and desiring to attend a different class.

These social structure issues can be eased by offering fellowship opportunities outside the Sunday class. Social events and fellowship opportunities should be provided to maintain existing relationships, while also providing additional opportunities for new contacts made in the elective setting to grow and mature.

Additional Costs

Electives require additional curricular materials. This is another disadvantage. The more classes you offer the more quarterlies and materials you must provide. Obviously, offering elective classes is not something to be done haphazardly or impulsively. Careful planning can make it work. The Sunday school committee should plan for the money and resources to be available in the church budget.

ADVANTAGES OF GROUPING BY ELECTIVE

Enthusiasm

One of the most significant benefits electives provide is the enthusiasm they generate among adults. Adults, as we have seen, are motivated in their learning efforts by a desire to meet specific needs or pursue special interests. Therefore, adults relish the opportunity to choose the topics that appeal to them or that will help them solve a real-life problem. This is very important to the personal and spiritual growth of adults. The fact that the adult has chosen the class and voluntarily attends means there will be a much higher motivation and more serious approach in study.

Departure From The Routine

Electives help break down routine and tradition. Routine and tradition are not problems in and of themselves, but when routine leads to boredom and tradition stifles more effective learning arrangements they become problems.

Social Interaction

Electives break up cliques. As we have mentioned, long-existing social relationships among adults in the Sunday school is a common thing. And like routine and tradition, they are not necessarily bad. However, it is common for some adults to settle for their close circle of acquaintances and never reach out to form new friendships. Even worse, some cliques are so tight that adults who are new to the church may find it impossible to penetrate them. The elective system, with its frequently changing class memberships, encourages new contacts between adults.

Sense of Achievement

Electives give adults a sense of achievement. This is particularly true of courses that offer a substantial challenge and relate to gaining relevant skills, such as parenting and marriage enrichment. When a person completes a course of study he feels a sense of accomplishment and satisfaction, such as one feels in earning a diploma.

New Teacher Recruitment

An elective system strengthens the Sunday school's teaching staff. First, the increase in classes offered requires the Sunday school to enlist and train more teachers. In the long run, this is good for the church.

Second, with class assignments being temporary and usually short-term, it is much easier to enlist new teachers. Many people appreciate the fact they can accept an assignment without feeling they have been trapped into a lifetime commitment.

Third, regular teachers are afforded opportunities to take time off. A teacher needs time to recharge spiritually, mentally, and emotionally by attending Sunday school classes and/or a teacher-training class.

Finally, we should not overlook the advantage of the student being exposed to several different teachers over time. This brings freshness to the adult's Sunday school experience, as well as varied insights into the Christian faith.

SUMMARY

As an individual, the adult has specific interests and needs. He also needs to feel he belongs to a significant support group. The adult Sunday school program addresses these needs effectively.

From the earliest days of the Church, Christians have been instructed to gather for fellowship and to share with one another those things they find in common.

> "They devoted themselves to the apostles' teaching and to the fellowship, to the breaking of bread and to prayer" Acts 2:42.

"Let us consider how we may spur one another on toward love and good deeds. Let us not give up meeting together, as some are in the habit of doing, but let us encourage one another—and all the more as you see the Day approaching" (Hebrews 10:24,25).

This can be done within a positive setting, in a learning environment with peers. The grouping alternatives we have discussed in this chapter help us to accomplish these goals in a more effective way. Both age-grouping and elective approaches offer advantages and disadvantages. These must be weighed with consideration to your students and your educational goals.

Planning— The Key to Success

Successful teaching is not accidental; it comes by careful planning. That does not demean the role of God's Spirit or a teacher's gifts; but all things being equal, a gifted teacher who is careless about planning will not do as well as a less gifted teacher who applies an effective lesson plan.

THE VALUE OF QUARTERLY PLANNING

Tragically, some teachers plan no further than next week's lesson. The wise teacher understands the value of gaining an overview of the whole quarter.

When you first receive your teacher's quarterly, take time to look through it. Familiarize yourself with the unit themes, the lesson titles, and the objectives. Take time also to survey the Scripture passages and key verses for each lesson.

By surveying the lessons for the quarter, you are better able to pace the study of the theme. Questions raised prematurely can be directed to future lessons that will look closely at the answer. You are also better able to prepare resource material for a particular lesson when you have several weeks to gather it.

At times it is helpful to know, not only what is coming up in the weeks ahead, but also what is planned quarters ahead. This can be valuable information for long-range planning such as for scheduling films and guest speakers, coordinating topics with home cells, and planning special class projects.

THE VALUE OF CURRICULUM

The word *curriculum* comes from a Latin word meaning "a running, a course, a race." It has come to mean a specific "course" of study. To educators, curriculum is not only *what* is taught but also *how* it is taught. To most Sunday school teachers it means their teacher's quarterly.

A teacher was heard to say, "We don't use curriculum; we teach the Bible!" What a tragic misunderstanding. *Every teacher* uses a curriculum because curriculum is the sum of what you teach and how you teach, whether or not you use a quarterly. The question is not should I use a curriculum, but what kind of curriculum am I using? Is my curriculum (my teaching) biblically sound, comprehensive, and well-balanced?

The intent of curriculum is to provide direction, and to avoid confusion or oversight. Remember the word's origin—a course for a race. Imagine the chaos and wasted effort in a marathon where every runner chose his own direction and distance. Neither should Bible study be haphazard, a hit-or-miss approach cannot provide a balanced understanding of God's Word. Systematic and comprehensive study is what builds mature saints.

The Bible is our textbook; curriculum is a tool for planning the lesson. Curriculum is the starting point, not the finished product. Its purpose is to insure orderly coverage of the Bible's truths. Its value is that it makes the teacher's work much less stressful and time consuming. Keep in mind that no curriculum can teach, only people can teach. Much more than the quarterly, the teacher is the key to success. A caring and knowledgeable teacher, anointed by God, determines the tone and success of a class. A well-planned curriculum makes you even more effective.

THE VALUE OF WEEKLY LESSON PLANNING

Planning is part of our attempt to cooperate more intelligently with God. It is not a rejection of the supernatural, nor is it a hindrance to God's Spirit. After all, if God prepared the plan of salvation before the foundations of the world were laid (Ephesians 1:4; 1 Peter 1:20), certainly His Spirit can guide you in planning your session ahead of time. While every teacher eventually senses the need for impromptu teaching in response to expressed needs, the fact remains—planning is the key to success. "To fail to plan is to plan to fail!"

In *First Steps for Teachers* Bill Martin lists several reasons why you should use a weekly lesson plan:[27]

1. *Planning provides unity and continuity in teaching.* As a result of planning our lessons will flow smoothly from previous and to future lessons. This also prevents wasting time with secondary or nonrelated issues.

2. *Planning helps discipline the teacher.* When a teacher is ill-prepared there is a temptation to take shortcuts or ramble. Unfortunately, this usually results in shallow teaching that has little focus or insight. Planning requires the teacher to study and research.

3. *Planning makes the presentation more interesting.* A teacher has time to secure resources, choose creative methods, and find interesting stories, things that mean the difference between a boring lesson and an exciting one.

4. *Planning builds teacher confidence.* Following a well-designed lesson plan almost always makes class session more interesting and productive. Students will be more attentive and more involved. As a result the teacher will have a greater sense of accomplishment and proficiency.

FIVE COMPONENTS OF LESSON PLANNING

There are five areas of concern in planning your weekly lesson. The following questions direct the teacher to these five components of lesson planning.

What Is The Lesson's Main Idea?

The main idea is the theme of the lesson, and is usually indicated in the lesson title. A good grasp of the main idea is important because it sets the boundaries for the lesson. It helps you see how the lesson relates to the overall unit theme. It also helps prevent slipping into "off the subject" discussions.

The beginning of class is always critical. The teacher must grab the student's attention quickly, focusing interest on the lesson's main idea and leading into the Bible study. One way to do this is to start the class by presenting a common problem and building anticipation of resolution in today's study. You might pose a difficult, thought-provoking question and suggest that today's lesson will help the class find God's wisdom on this matter. Using current events to introduce your main idea is timely and usually will grab attention. Brainstorming, agree-disagree statements, skits, role-play, interviews, and sentence completion are all effective methods to use to focus your adults on the lesson.

What Is My Lesson Objective?

The dictionary defines an objective as "the aim or end of an action; a point to be hit or reached." In teaching, an objective is, "A statement which describes what the students will know, feel, or do after we have taught them." The teacher must move in a specific, predetermined direction to reach his target.

Awareness of adult developmental needs is closely related. We must not forget that learning requires change, and change happens in three areas.

1. Cognitive learning: changes in knowledge

2. Affective learning: changes in attitudes

3. Psycho-motor learning: changes in conduct

Therefore, our lesson objective should fall within three categories: knowing, feeling, and doing objectives.

Objectives in Christian education go beyond those of secular education, which are primarily concerned with what the student knows or is able to do. The ultimate goal for the Sunday school teacher is to help people mature in Christ and become faithful, productive members of the Church. This means we must be concerned with life application and how the student feels.

Perhaps the most common weakness in Sunday schools is

teachers teaching without a clear objective. A suggested objective is usually provided in your curricular materials, but your teaching can improve greatly by learning to write your own lesson objectives. Good lesson objectives are brief enough to be remembered, clear enough to be written down, and specific enough to be attainable.

Do you target your teaching? The value of a good lesson objective cannot be overemphasized. Someone has well said, "Aim at nothing and you are sure to hit it." To aim is to target your teaching. You are trying to define a statement that clarifies your direction for the day.

What Teaching Activities Will I Use?

After you understand the main idea and you have specified your objective, planning should turn to teaching activities. Teaching activities are those actions of the student and the teacher designed to bring better understanding of a particular idea.

Keep the emphasis on activity. Don't ask yourself, "What am I going to say (or do) in class?" Instead ask, "What am I and the students going to do together to better understand this idea?" Answering that question leads directly to thinking about activities and methods.

Remember, the more the student's five senses are involved in the learning process the more rapid and effective the learning. The more the student is involved the greater the learning.

What Resources Will I Need?

The fourth step in lesson planning is to consider resources. Resources are those tools and equipment used by the teacher and the student to carry out the teaching methods and activities. A resource is something that helps you demonstrate, explain, or clarify an idea, process, or fact. Numerous resources are available to you for meeting your lesson objectives. Some examples are paper and pencils, overhead projector and screen, cassette tapes and recorder, video recorder and monitor, maps, charts, posters, filmstrips, chalkboard, bulletin board, etc.

Before Sunday morning you should list of all the resources you will need for your lesson. Make arrangements with your Sunday school superintendent or other responsible persons to have the equipment in your classroom Sunday morning.

What Is My Evaluation Of This Lesson Plan?

Evaluation is a very important part of becoming a skillful teacher. To assist in evaluating the lesson plan you have put together ask yourself the following questions. Are the main ideas and objectives directly related? Have a variety of methods and activities been planned? What kinds of questions will be asked during the class? Have I made spiritual preparations for this lesson? Answering these questions will force you to look at your lesson preparation with a critical eye. Flaws and oversights will become apparent. This kind of evaluation is imperative.

A day or two after the class you can evaluate the class session by answering these questions: Did my opening remarks or activities grab student attention and interest? Did everything move along smoothly? Was the material presented logically and clearly? Did the teaching activities and methods work well?

Beyond the evaluation of the lesson plan you will also want to consider evaluating yourself as a teacher. Self-evaluation is not usually very productive or accurate. Ask your pastor or a teacher with some expertise to evaluate your teaching skill. Some teachers have even asked their students to evaluate them. None of us enjoy being evaluated. It is threatening and ego deflating. But it is essential if weaknesses are to be identified and improvements made. If your mind is open and your heart is sincere, evaluation can be a positive experience. "Whoever gives heed to instruction prospers, and blessed is he who trusts in the Lord" (Proverbs 16:20).

DEVELOP A WEEKLY PLANNING SCHEDULE

What are some of the bad planning habits teachers typically develop? One is the Saturday-night planner who spends one panic-filled hour late Saturday night trying to absorb the quarterly and figure out the teaching activities. These teachers are easily recognizable on Sunday morning by the dark circles under their eyes and their sloth-like manner.

The TV planner studies the quarterly while watching television. The length of actual planning time depends on their interest in the program. However, most of the planning is done during commercials while simultaneously trying to open a 7-UP and a bag of potato chips.

The on-the-run planner jots down notes on the back of envelopes or scraps of paper while racing through the week. He relies on a good memory, but sometimes forgets to bring the paper scraps on Sunday morning.

Then there is the good-intentions planner. He begins lesson planning early in the week with high hopes—a good start! But he often becomes a Saturday-night planner by not getting back to planning during the week.

The point is PLANNING TAKES TIME. You will never use your full potential as a teacher if you don't set aside quality time for planning. The following is a suggested weekly planning schedule. If you have had trouble developing good planning habits, try this schedule and see if it helps you.

Monday

Planning should begin with these four steps. First, start with prayer. Ask the Holy Spirit to bring your heart and your mind to full alertness and sensitivity. Note the lesson theme and objective. Read the key Scripture verses listed in the lesson.

Second, read the entire lesson at one sitting. Don't try to remember everything. Your goal is an overview of the content.

Third, after reading the lesson write your personal lesson objective. In one statement, answer the following question: "What do I want the students to know, to feel, or to do as a result of this lesson?" Be specific. If your objective is too general you will not know if it has been reached.

Finally on Monday, memorize the outline's main points. Memorizing these main points early in the week will help you move smoothly through the lesson on Sunday.

Tuesday

Reread the lesson, marking the places you feel need emphasis. Most published curriculums supply more material than you can use in one class. Be selective; you know your student's needs. Focus on what will be relevant and helpful to them. Next, review the teaching activities provided in your curriculum. Consider developing your own activities to increase student involvement.

Wednesday

Arrange and outline your lesson presentation. Estimate the time needed for each segment. Then gather the materials and equipment you will need. The rest of the week you can continue to review your lesson plan and pray for the class.

There are several benefits to having your lesson planning done by Wednesday. You escape the pressure of last minute preparations. You have several days to discover fresh and relevant material from magazines, current news, and your own experiences. And you have time for the lesson to "soak in" to your heart and mind, allowing for a relaxed and natural presentation. Your students will notice and enjoy the class much more.

Increasing Adult Involvement in Learning

10

Many a teacher has suffered the agony of standing before a class of unresponsive and inattentive students. It is not a pleasant experience. It can leave a teacher feeling frustrated and even guilty. True teaching is very difficult, if not impossible, under such circumstances.

The teacher is not the only one to suffer, however. Students are affected in a much more serious way because learning is not taking place. In his book, *Learning Together*, Ron Held observes, "Learning is not a passive experience; it is an active process. It is not something that happens to the pupil; it is something he does. The difference...is the difference between the spectator in the stands and the athlete out on the field or court. One is only looking on; the other is actively involved."[28] Learning is proportional to involvement. Good teaching involves students, the more a student is involved the more rapidly and effectively he will learn. The question is, "How can we increase involvement?"

STRATEGIES FOR GREATER INVOLVEMENT

Address Adult Interests And Needs

We can increase adult involvement by addressing their interests and their needs. Adults ask themselves, "Is this relevant to my life?" If they decide it is not, you have lost them. A student's attendance should not always be interpreted as interest in the lesson. Adults attend Sunday school for different reasons. For many, fellowship is a greater motivation than learning. While Sunday school should provide social interaction, education must also be one of our priorities. If adults are attending only for social reasons you must discover ways to involve them in active learning. Show them how the lesson topic relates to their needs and their interests. Only then will they be motivated to involve themselves.

Challenge Their Minds

We can increase student involvement by challenging their minds. People love a challenge, something that puts their intellect to the test. Adults no longer have the need, nor do they desire, to be spoon fed. If your students are bored, they may be under challenged. Give them thought-provoking questions that require some thinking to answer. Don't ask questions answerable with a simple "yes" or "no" or "pat" answer. Don't be afraid to let them do their own investigation, to use research materials, to find answers to their problems, and to come to personal decisions.

Use A Variety Of Learning Activities

We can increase student involvement by offering them a variety of learning activities in which to participate. The two worst misconceptions about teaching are "talking is teaching" and "listening is learning." Many teachers would not agree with these ideas, nevertheless they act as if they do. The teacher does all the talking while the students passively listen. Unfortunately, people have little tolerance of this teaching style. They may look attentive, but their minds are miles away. Involve students in the learning process as much as possible by means of teaching methods and learning activities. Many such activities are often provided in your teacher's quarterly.

Cultivate A Climate Conducive To Interaction

Teachers can increase student involvement by designing an environment conducive to interaction. First, by giving adults freedom to express themselves. If students believe their comments will be ridiculed they will keep quiet. Your task is creating an atmosphere of acceptance and mutual respect. Ask yourself, "Do my students feel secure enough in my class to join in?"

Then consider the physical environment. It is easier for people to share when they are seated in a circle or a semicircle. If the class is smaller, consider sitting with them rather than standing above them. Other concerns would be, Is the room well lit? Is the temperature comfortable? Are the students preoccupied with being too cold, or too hot? Is the room cheerfully decorated? Do the students feel comfortable and at ease?

Be patient but persistent. Expect student involvement, and let your students know you do; but not by threats or by pleading. Let your expectation be implied by your smile and warm appreciation when someone does participate.

TEACHING ACTIVITIES INVOLVE ADULTS

Teaching activities are those actions of the student and the teacher designed to bring a better understanding of a particular idea. Teachers often ask themselves, "What am I going to do in class next Sunday?" This approach is centered on the teacher. Perhaps the more important question is, "What are my students going to do in class?" The latter question forces the teacher to consider the student's predicament. Will the adults sit motionless, listening to me drone on for an hour? Or, will they be actively engaged in activities that bring them a better understanding of the lesson topic? Of the strategies to promote adult involvement listed above, thoughtful use of teaching methods is perhaps the most effective.

Jesus used a variety of teaching methods. A review of the Gospels shows His use of field trips, storytelling, lecture, question and answer, demonstration and discussion, not to mention visual aids. As the Master Teacher, Jesus knew His words would have greater impact if they were reinforced with appropriate methods and activities. Everything His disciples heard, saw, touched, or encountered intensified the learning experience.

When Jesus healed the man born blind He used the opportunity to teach, "I am the light of the world" (John 9). He raised Lazarus from the dead and taught, "I am the resurrection and the life. He who believes in me will live, even though he dies; and whoever lives and believes in me will never die" (John 11). When He fed the 5,000, He proclaimed, "I am the bread of life. He who comes to me will never go hungry" (John 6).

Good teachers are always on the watch for new ideas. Even the most creative teachers will confess that many of their methods came from observing others. If you never observe creative teachers chances are you will never be a creative teacher, just as never being exposed to great art limits chances of developing into a great painter. Draw from your experience; what methods impressed you as a student? What activities were effective? Visit other churches and Sunday school classes to see what methods they are using. Teacher training seminars are a good source of new ideas. Find out what other teachers have done to bring variety and involvement to the classroom.

Keeping an idea file is a good practice. New ideas are likely to be forgotten before you have a chance to use them. Ideas, news clippings, interesting anecdotes, and other potentially useful items that you cannot use right away can be filed for future use. When you need to inject new life into your teaching style, review your idea file. Even if a filed item is not used, the review process may generate ideas and solutions to your teaching problems.

Choosing Teaching Activities

When using teaching methods and activities, keep in mind the following guidelines developed by Donald Griggs. They are designed to help you successfully use teaching activity in your classroom.[29]

1. *Use activities that involve as many students in an active way as possible.* Your goal is broad-based involvement. Don't use activities that appeal only to a small group.

2. *Use activities in which you have some confidence.* If you do not thoroughly understand the activity and how it works, it probably won't.

3. *Use activities that encourage students to use their imagination and creativity.* You might even allow students to help plan activities.

4. *Don't bore students with overly used activities.* The idea of creating interest and variety is lost if you use the same activities week after week. Students will soon tire of them and resist involvement.

5. *Give students time to become acquainted with new activities.* If your activity does not work the first time it may mean students need time to experiment and become comfortable with the activity. Be patient; in time it may become a popular and helpful activity.

6. *Use activities that contribute directly to reaching the lesson goal.* Activity simply for activity sake is a bad idea.

7. *Use activities that lead students to seek answers, state conclusions or express creative responses.* Students will be much more impressed (educationally speaking) by conclusions they arrive at themselves than by those merely recited by the teacher.

INVOLVEMENT EXPERIENCES FOR SPIRITUAL GROWTH

Perry Downs has identified four types of involvement experience vital to spiritual growth.[30] Teachers should strive to incorporate as many of these experiences as possible into the learning experiences of adults.

Interaction With The Content Of The Word

Because Christianity is based on a faith that has content to be known, interaction with that content is essential to spiritual development. This is why the Apostle Paul first prayed the Colossians would be "fill(ed)...with the knowledge of his will" so they might "grow in the knowledge of God" (Colossians 1:9, 10). Paul instructed his readers so that they could be mature. Knowledge and maturity are not the same, but it is impossible for a person to be spiritually mature and yet be ignorant of spiritual truth.

In the classroom, use teaching methods and techniques that encourage interaction with the Word. The Bereans were reported to be of noble character because "they received the message with great eagerness and examined the Scriptures every day to see if what Paul said was true" (Acts 17:11). The teacher's ambition should not be to report what the Bible says, but to equip adults to use God's Word themselves as their personal guide to faith and conduct. Paul urged Timothy, "Do your best to present yourself to God as one approved, a workman who does not need to be ashamed and who correctly handles the word of truth" (2 Timothy 2:15). The Sunday school teacher seeks to help this become true of his or her students.

Involvement In The Body Of Christ

Like parts of the human body, the members of Christ's body are linked together. Paul made this point in 1 Corinthians 12, "The body is a unit, though it is made up of many parts; and though all its parts are many, they form one body. So it is with Christ.... Now you are the body of Christ, and each one of you is a part of it" (verses 12,27).

Spiritual growth is a process that takes place over time as a result of interaction with other Christians and participation in Christian service. In other words, the primary context for spiritual growth and learning is within the body of Christ. Without involvement in the fellowship of believers, adults cannot develop spiritually as they should.

Believers are not isolated, we influence one another and care for one another. Speaking of the body of Christ, Paul said "its parts should have equal concern for each other. If one part suffers, every part suffers with it; if one part is honored, every part rejoices with it." (1 Corinthians 12:25–26). Christian education must include opportunities for this type of interaction as part of its curriculum. This is necessary for Christ's Church to be built up. "From him the whole body, joined and held together by every supporting ligament, grows and builds itself up in love, as each part does its work" (Ephesians 4:16).

Exposure To Models

Adults also need to be exposed to models of Christian maturity. This is part of the discipleship process. As we interact with more mature Christians we observe and begin to adopt their attitudes and values. We see how they deal with the problems of life. In time, we become more and more like them. Jesus had this in mind when He said, "A student is not above his teacher, but everyone who is fully trained will be like his teacher" (Luke 6:40).

If we want students to reach spiritual maturity, and if students become like their teacher, then the teacher must be a model of spiritual maturity. However, the models we put before adults can be either literary or flesh and blood. The study of Christian men and women of God, both from Scripture and Church history, can inspire adults to follow their lead. But in some way students must "see" examples of what the Bible is talking about. Concepts, such as faith, love, and humility, are hard to understand, but they come alive when we see them lived out in others.

Dialogue With Other Believers

Dialogue with other believers is the fourth type of involvement experience adults need for spiritual growth. Jesus had extensive conversations and dialogues with His disciples and others. Paul did the same. Dialogue was a major part of teaching in that time of history.

Modern study of adult learning also suggests that because adults are reasoning and thinking people, interaction is essential. Why then do we so often see teachers talking and students listening? Is true spiritual growth possible if someone only comes, listens, and leaves?

In the classroom, use teaching methods that allow adults to interact with the teacher and with each other. As adults share the wisdom they have gleaned from their life experiences, their struggles and their victories others are able to learn. They will change how they think, how they feel, and subsequently how they live. This is what learning is all about. Teaching methods and activities are valuable because they help us to accomplish that involvement.

If your teaching style has been primarily lecture, or if you have been afraid to try other methods, work to expand your repertoire. There is a great variety of teaching methods and activities from which to choose. Your class will be greatly enhanced as you incorporate methods that motivate and involve adults.

Teaching Methods for Adults

11

LECTURE METHODS

The lecture is the most commonly used teaching method in adult classrooms. Teachers are comfortable with it be cause they like the security of being in control. But students target the lecture as the most boring method. The question is when to lecture and when not to lecture.

A weakness of lectures is the teacher-centered, teacher-directed format it brings to the classroom. Lack of student participation is a problem inherent with lecture. Lectures may also present material more rapidly than students can comprehend it. So pace your lecture, giving students mental rest periods by means of illustrations, questions, and brief pauses.

The teacher's body and voice control are also important. A monotone lecture can be an agonizing experience! A good lecturer speaks clearly with varying pitch and volume. He also moves about using natural gestures.

Some techniques for minimizing student boredom include the following: (1) a pretest to stimulate interest in the lecture subject; (2) an outline of your lecture on the chalkboard or on a worksheet; (3) taped interviews or other material to play during the lecture; (4) index cards containing Scripture verses, illustrations, or interesting facts to be read aloud by assigned students at different points during the lecture.

Despite its weaknesses, the lecture is effective in certain situations. It can quickly present material in an organized way, clarify problems, and analyze viewpoints. It can be used to stimulate, inspire, and challenge; and also maintain control over classroom activity. The lecture is also useful for large groups when other techniques are not feasible.

Be mindful of its weaknesses, but don't discard the lecture method merely in an attempt to be creative. Using the techniques presented here will increase student appreciation for the lecture. The following are other teaching methods that can be used with the lecture to help sustain student interest.

Symposium

A symposium is two or more people giving mini-lectures, about 5 minutes apiece, related to the lesson topic. The speakers generally sit at a table facing the class. A moderator introduces the topic and speakers, each of whom present a different aspect of the subject. The moderator may also direct a question and answer period following the speakers' presentations.

Your students can use this method effectively if given enough time and instruction to prepare adequately. The symposium can be effective when (1) the class needs concise information; (2) it is important to spotlight key issues or various viewpoints; and (3) you want different speakers to add variety to the material.

Listening Teams

Listening teams evaluate what they hear from a guest lecturer, a research report, a video or a film. Use listening teams when important ideas might go unnoticed or when several sides of a question need attention. After the presentation the teams should each share their findings or observations with the class.

You can form listening teams by grouping students within the class and assigning each group with a specific list of things to listen for in the presentation, or perhaps each group could be given a question to be answered from the material presented.

Research Report

Research reports are generally presented by someone other than the teacher, usually students. The teacher should assign reports to individuals or small groups 2 or 3 weeks ahead of time. The reporter(s) can go to a public or church library, conduct interviews, or carry out surveys to gather material.

Assignments may pertain to any topic determined by the teacher, a theological doctrine, a Bible character, a contemporary social issue, a biblical or contemporary occupation, custom, or circumstance, etc. Students might visit a prison or nursing home and report how the class might minister to those in need.

It is important for the teacher to give clear instructions to ensure the students find and report information that contributes toward reaching the lesson objective.

Guest Lecturer

Use guest lecturers who have experiences and knowledge about the lesson topic. During a study of Paul's journeys, ask a missionary to discuss the problems of foreign languages, customs, and travel. For a lesson on healing, a doctor could speak concerning the complexity of the human body and the wisdom of God's design. A Christian lawyer or city official might lecture on the role of the Christian in government.

A guest lecturer is more effective if enough time is given for questions and answers. Suggestions may be given to the guest lecturer on ways of involving the students in discussion.

Demonstration

A great benefit of the demonstration is its visual impact, through which the teacher can communicate a great amount of material. This method can be used to present biblical customs, clothing, architecture, and cultural designs, or to show how something in a Scripture passage might have been done. The demonstration can use many individuals and reveal talents that otherwise might be left dormant and undiscovered.

DISCUSSION METHODS

Agree-Disagree

The agree-disagree activity is a thought-provoking polling of opinions. It is not meant to answer a question or to solve a problem, rather it is intended to stimulate interest and discussion. For this reason, the statements used *must not* have a right or wrong answer. You are polling opinions on matters for which differences of opinion are entirely appropriate. Remember, the goal is to stimulate discussion, not to have half the students feel they have answered wrong.

Prepare a few thought-provoking statements, each phrased to force a judgment based on personal opinion. There should be no right or wrong response, so the teacher must be prepared to discuss both sides of the issue. Students are asked to quickly mark on paper their agreement or disagreement for each statement. Marking their response prevents vacillation and peer pressure from interfering with the activity.

By a show of hands tally the results and discuss those statements producing the closest division of opinion, these have the greatest discussion potential. Ask a volunteer to explain why he agreed with the statement, then ask someone who disagreed to respond. Alternate in this fashion as long as the discussion proves beneficial. The discussion does not need to be long since it is intended only to peak interest and lead into the study.

Brainstorming

Brainstorming is an activity that stimulates creative thinking about a given problem or question. It is often used to introduce a problem or a question that will be addressed in the lesson. Write a question or a problem on the overhead projector or chalkboard. Ask students to suggest rapid-fire answers or solutions. It is important that these be given quickly. The greatest advantage of brainstorming is that the ideas are not evaluated at this point. All responses are welcome. This encourages openness and creativity. The quicker the ideas come, the better. If you have an extremely large group, you may want to break into smaller groups for several brainstorming sessions. It is probably good to limit the brainstorming session to a 3- to 5-minute period. If the flow of ideas is strong, a possible extension is in order.

It is important that each suggestion be listed by a member of the group. It is even better if these are listed in everyone's view on the chalkboard or overhead screen. Following the brainstorming, evaluate the ideas shared. These can be developed more fully later in the session.

Buzz Groups

Buzz groups are 6 to 10 students in discussion for a short period. It is an extremely flexible teaching activity that can be used to discuss a Scripture passage, identify problems, explore issues, propose solutions, evaluate answers, or share experiences. They can be used at any point in the lesson.

Buzz groups offer three benefits. First, buzz groups encourage students to think, to become involved. Many adults are reluctant to verbalize their thoughts before a large group. Yet in a small group they find the self-confidence to join the conversation. It is important for adults to share their experience and knowledge. They need to feel needed, and feel that their contributions help make a difference.

Second, buzz groups interject variety and activity into the class, helping students avoid the sleepy monotony of listening to a one-voice, uninterrupted lecture. They also help create an atmosphere of informality, important to adult learning. Adults discover answers for themselves.

Third, buzz groups relieve the teacher of the pressure to "carry" the class. Rather than mechanically dispensing truth, the teacher helps students learn together. Students share the responsibility for the class.

Each buzz group should have a leader. He is not to teach, nor is he to monopolize the discussion; his task is to prevent conversational traffic jams, keep the group on the subject and encourage everyone's participation. The teacher may choose to give each leader brief written instructions, including the questions or statements to be discussed. Groups may discuss the same topics or be assigned different ones.

Each group should also select a secretary to write down the main points of the discussion. This person should be prepared to give a concise report to the whole class when it reassembles. If you have a large class, you may want to have reports from a sampling of groups. Following these reports the teacher should summarize, draw conclusions, or otherwise pull together the efforts of the different groups.

Film or Video Talkback

In the talk-back activity, students respond to the information or message given in a film, a filmstrip, or a videotape presentation. It is helpful to give students the questions that are to be answered or discussed following the showing of the material. This activity can be adapted to a listening-team approach. Three or four individuals are given the responsibility of looking for particular things in the presentation. After the presentation has been given, each member of the listening-team shares the information he has discovered. The discussion is then opened to the entire group. The film talk-back and the listening-team approach are the same, except that one is designed for individuals while the other is designed for teams.

Neighbor Nudging

Neighbor nudging is a fun technique where two students interact briefly and intensely on a particular discussion question. The idea is that you, figuratively speaking, reach over and nudge the person beside you and get him involved in the discussion. The discussion is limited to 1 or 2 minutes. The time limit encourages involvement and quick thinking. The teacher may or may not call for comments after this discussion. This method involves everyone and works well in stationary seating arrangements because moving the chairs is unnecessary.

Panel

The panel presents information by a group of experts. The panel members and the leader should get together before the session to determine exactly what is expected of them. During the presentation, the panel members sit facing the class. The teacher or leader of the session presents a question for discussion and gives each panel member an opportunity to respond. Then the class takes turns asking questions of the panel members. When the questions are directed to a specific individual, he responds first, and then others may respond as they choose.

Question and Answer

Question and answer is the teacher's chief means of directing class discussion and stimulating thought. Questions were a method Jesus used to provoke thought about the most crucial issues of life. The Gospels record over 100 of His questions.

A good reason to plan time for questions and answers throughout a lecture is that questions raise curiosity and interest. This will involve students giving them a sense of participation, the class will becomes theirs, not just the teacher's.

Use questions to bridge the gap between the theoretical and the practical, between faith and practice. Use them to focus on the implications and applications of abstract truths such as love, forgiveness, faith, and hope. Use questions as an evaluation tool to discover how well we have communicated, and how much students have retained.

There are three general categories of teaching questions. *Identification questions* ask, "What do you know? They help reveal what the student knows or how well you have communicated. *Analytical questions* ask, "What do you think?" They seek a judgment or an analysis by the student because he is not asked to merely "parrot" facts. He is encouraged to deal creatively with what he has learned. *Value questions* ask, "How do you feel?" These require self examination and sometimes exposure of personal thoughts or feelings, forcing students to think through their values and their attitudes.

Use the following guidelines for asking questions.

1. Plan to vary the kind and the difficulty of your questions.

2. Give the students adequate time to think and to respond.

3. Be affirming in responding to the student's answers.

4. "Why" and "how" questions are more effective because they cannot be answered with a simple "yes" or "no."

Well-designed and well-timed questions are crucial to classroom success, but they require skill and planning. A wise teacher will invest the time and make the effort to include thought-provoking questions in his lesson plan.

DRAMA METHODS

Role-play

A role-play is an extemporaneous acting out of a common situation or problem with the intent that the participants discover solutions or gain understanding. Several volunteers play the roles of the characters involved in a problem. They are usually given a few minutes to plan their presentation within the guidelines of the written instructions.

After discussing the setting, the players return and act out the problem for the entire group. The enactment should be realistic but exaggerated to bring out the characteristics of the roles they have been given. When a climactic moment is reached, the leader stops the action. This requires a sense of timing because you do not want to overplay the situation.

Role-play is usually followed by discussion. The players can express how they felt in the roles they were assigned. Did the experience give them new insights that could be applied to life? How could Scriptural principles have been applied to prevent or to alleviate the problem? What lessons can we learn about how to better handle these situations? The teacher should summarize the results of the exercise.

Skits

The skit is a dramatization similar to the role-play. In the skit, however, a formalized script is followed. The script is designed to illustrate one point or message, such as a biblical truth. The participants memorize their lines and then present the skit following the memorized script. Props are prepared ahead of time.

This is an excellent means of communicating a truth or illustrating and summarizing the lesson truth of the day. Always keep in mind the specific goals of the lesson and, if possible, include these goals in the script. The script should also provide some statements for discussion following the skit presentation. After the skit has been given, you may use the feelings generated by it to start a discussion. Specific life-application lessons are necessary for learning to occur.

AUDIOVISUAL METHODS

When sight and hearing combine, each sense reinforces the other, greatly improving learning and retention. Audiovisual reinforcement is important. Adults live in a media world, exposed everyday to sophisticated use of media. They have come to think in terms of audiovisual learning.

Audiovisual tools are not in themselves a guarantee of an effective lesson. But, like other teaching methods, if used properly they will increase the effectiveness of your presentation.

Audiocassette

The cassette tape recorder is a versatile tool for the classroom. It could bring a guest speaker to your class without the expense of travel costs. Commercially produced tapes offer teaching or information on various subjects. You could also produce your own tape, perhaps an interview of someone from the congregation or community. "On-the-street" interviews with passersby would bring interest to a lecture. Interview a doctor, lawyer, counselor, public educator, or someone representing a trade, occupation, or issue in your community. You might even arrange to tape a telephone interview with someone of interest across the nation, or mail tapes from class-sponsored missionaries to maintain fresh interest in a missions work. Recordings will bring interest and excitement to your lesson.

Attention spans are short, even for adults, so use tapes for short periods only. A rule is a maximum of 10 minutes. For longer tapes, discuss what has been heard then play another segment.

Audiocassette tapes are useful outside the classroom also. Record the class session for shut-ins or senior citizens unable to attend. Use them to evaluate the strengths and the weaknesses of your presentation. Ask questions such as, "What audio improvements could I make in my speech clarity, vocabulary, or enunciation?" "Are my ideas comprehensible?" "Is the lesson's main thought being communicated well?" "How was the class discussion?" "What might I have done to make the discussion better?"

Slide-Tape Presentation

A slide-tape presentation could be used to illustrate the biblical truth of a lesson. The slide-tape presentation requires much work, but the students learn as they are working. Learning by doing is always effective.

Use the slide-tape presentation to illustrate a theme. Take the words of a song, such as "How Great Thou Art," and depict these in a pictorial way. Bible verses, contemporary social issues, or promotional themes can be given the same treatment. It may be best to consider how slides will be coordinated before they are taken. Write the script and then take pictures to accompany and to visualize the ideas. Your presentation is limited only by your creativity.

Chalkboard

The chalkboard is the "work horse" of learning aids. Its strength is immediate, spontaneous, and relatively effortless visual expression of an abstract idea. You can write words, present numbers, draw graphs or maps, or scribble your own doodling; anything to help you communicate your ideas. Turning to the chalkboard is sometimes all that is needed to arouse interest from a class. Some teachers have a tendency to talk to the chalkboard while writing. That may make it difficult for everyone to hear you; so generally it is best not to talk while writing. Also, be sure to write large enough so each word is clearly readable. When used correctly, the chalkboard can greatly increase the retention and speed of learning. It provides a visual impact in a very inexpensive and simple way.

Maps

Maps are an indispensable Bible study tool. They help us visualize the relationships of biblical places and events. Bible maps can be bought through many Christian bookstores. You may want to purchase large and durable maps of Bible lands to be mounted on the wall or in flip-chart fashion on an accompanying tripod. A more convenient alternative would be to buy a set of map transparencies for use on overhead projectors.

Overhead Projector

The overhead projector—the electronic chalkboard—is superior to the chalkboard because you can face your class while using it, giving you eye contact with your students. When drawing attention to something projected on the screen do not turn your back to the class, use a pencil laid on the transparency as a pointer. This keeps you facing the class. An advantage over filmstrips and slides is that it can be used while the room lights remain on. Again, you can have vital eye contact.

You can use an overhead for many purposes, such as displaying maps, listing the main points of your lesson, summarizing important truths, and presenting important facts or statistics. When using the overhead always print, don't use cursive. A printed word will be much clearer and easier to read than a word written in script. Use different colored pens for emphasis.

The overhead projector is an attention grabber. For that reason, turn it off when you no longer need it, otherwise it will distract students or compete for their attention. It is a good habit to place your material on the projector before turning it on, and to turn it off before removing transparencies. If you have a list of items on your transparency, use a sheet of paper to expose the points one at a time as you talk. This focuses attention on your point and prevents the class from getting ahead of you.

Prepare your overhead transparencies ahead of time for more efficient use of class time. In preparing overhead transparencies, ask yourself these questions: Is this visual worth making? Do the visual and verbal commentary complement each other? Is there good visibility? To whom or for whose benefit is the visual aimed?

Videos & Films

Many commercially produced videos and films are available on a wide range of subjects, both secular and Christian. The full length of a video or just relevant excerpts easily can be incorporated into the study of related Bible topics.

Always preview the video or film and make sure it is in working condition, meets the needs of your class, and does not contain any offensive or inappropriate material. You will usually want to follow up the video's key ideas or points with some type of interaction, which is another reason to be familiar with it's content ahead of time.

Don't overlook the home video recorder as a tool for Christian education. You or someone in your class can tape segments from news broadcasts, TV specials or documentaries, even scenes from situation comedies or other programs. These can serve to illustrate a problem, provoke thinking on social issues, introduce a topic, or present information relevant to your study.

Reaching Adults Through Christian Education

12

Have you ever asked yourself, "Will good people (unbelievers) make it to heaven?" We ask ourselves such questions because: (1) we naturally like good people and do not cherish the thought of any one's damnation, (2) we overlook or misunderstand the reality and consequence of man's sinful nature; or (3) we unconsciously want to ease our conscience from the responsibility of winning them to Christ.

A teacher's objective is to nurture spiritual growth. But nurturing saints must not contribute to the neglect of evangelizing sinners. Education, edification, and evangelism are the three-fold goals of Christian education. Even when the majority of students are Christian, a teacher must be evangelistic. Unsaved visitors deserve an opportunity to accept Christ.

Sunday schools grow in various ways, such as births, transfer of members from other churches, and migration of believers from other communities; yet growth by evangelism should be a major priority. Without evangelism the church and Sunday school will die. It has been said, the church that does not evangelize the lost will soon cease to evangelize its own sons and daughters.

In this chapter and the next, we will consider ways to improve outreach and assimilation in the adult class. We will look at two strategies for reaching your adult community. One is to train and encourage adults to use "relational evangelism" opportunities; the other is to give the adult Christian education program an outreach orientation.

RELATIONAL EVANGELISM

The Unchurched American Adult

The Princeton Religion Research Center (part of the Gallup organization) surveyed unchurched American adults in 1952, 1965, and 1978. Over half of those surveyed (52 percent) could image becoming fairly active in church if they could find a church meeting the following criteria:[31]

1. *A church that would listen to their religious doubts and spiritual needs*
2. *A church with vital worship and preaching*
3. *A church with a real thirst for Christian education*
4. *A church that will simply invite them to join*

In 1988, the same organization replicated the 1978 survey and found little change in the attitude of unchurched. The surveys revealed that Christians, in attempting to reach the unchurched, are not working in as hostile a climate as some might expect. Most of the unchurched have traditional religious backgrounds with 60 percent having attended church as a child. Seventy percent believe Jesus is divine, and 80 percent cite a religious preference. Sixty percent believe the Bible was inspired by God, and 80 percent say they sometimes pray to God.[32]

When asked to suggest circumstances that might lead to their increased attendance, 16 percent mentioned a life crisis and a church that demonstrated genuine interest in them. About the same number would be open to returning if invited by a member and they liked the people.[33]

These surveys suggest every church in America is surrounded by unchurched adults who would be receptive to a church or a Sunday school class that showed a genuine interest in their welfare. These findings make it all the more tragic that some churches retreat into a defensive mentality believing their community is unreceptive or hostile toward the church.

The Friendship Factor: Key To Evangelism

In his chapter, "Evangelization of Adults" in *The Christian Education of Adults*, Perry Downs identifies three approaches to evangelism.[34] Mass evangelism relies on lay people bringing friends to hear a professional evangelist share the gospel. Confrontational evangelism confronts a non-believer with his need of salvation, i.e., door-to-door and street corner campaigns.

There is no doubt that people are won to the Lord using these approaches. But evangelism is hindered when we think first in terms of massive multi-media campaigns, high-pressured and impersonal "sales" techniques, or something left to the "professionals" (evangelists, pastors, etc.). The Church is a living organism that grows best when each believer is an integral part of its outreach efforts.

The third approach is relational evangelism. Relational evangelism, sometimes called friendship evangelism, is just as intent on soul-winning as the others, but it is a more comfortable approach for most adults because it works within the structure and boundaries of a friendship. It is less confrontational and perceived as more genuine and caring than media campaigns or door-to-door witnessing.

Philip set the pattern for relational evangelism in John 1:44–46. After he found Jesus, he shared that news with Nathanael. When Nathanael hesitated, Philip responded, "Come and see." This invitation is at the heart of relational evangelism. We find relational evangelism in Mark 5 when the demoniac told his family the good news, and also in Luke 5 where Levi's contacts with tax collectors exposed them to Jesus. In John 1, "The first thing Andrew did was to find his brother Simon and tell him, 'We have found the Messiah.'" In Acts 10, Cornelius "called together his relatives and close friends" to hear the gospel. In Acts 16, Lydia shared her experience with the members of her household. The gospel travels naturally through the networks of close relationships, resulting in explosive growth.

Studies indicate that 70 percent of all people who accept Christ as Savior do so because of the direct influence of a friend or family member. Your adults know many Nathanaels—they have daily contact with neighbors, businessmen, store clerks, and unsaved family members. Relational evangelism is the strategy of identifying and using these relationships as avenues of evangelism.

As the term implies, relational evangelism must be based on a sincere relationship. It is not the manipulation or coercion of people into the church. Rather, our motivation is to know and to love others, helping them with their problems by introducing them to Jesus and to the fellowship of His people.

The Christian's Influence

"You are the light of the world...let your light shine before men, that they may see your good deeds and praise your Father in heaven" (Matthew 5:14–16). Christ intends for His people to influence others toward God. This is most naturally done through our contacts with unsaved friends.

Jesus set the example by befriending the lost and using those relationships to communicate God's love and salvation. Zacchaeus and the woman at the well are two examples. The self-righteous elite called Him a "friend of sinners." It's a matter of stewardship, for not only is time, talent, and treasure to be used for godly purposes, but also for our friendships. In fact, in the story of the shrewd manager (Luke 16) Jesus commended the use of position and possessions to win friends. Adults need to be taught the eternal value of using relationships to bring people to salvation.

The Holy Spirit can use a Christian's influence to provoke thought and, hopefully, to convict a friend of their need for Christ. This is the principle behind Paul's instruction regarding a marriage in which one spouse becomes a Christian while the other does not. "For the unbelieving husband has been sanctified through his wife, and the unbelieving wife has been sanctified through her believing husband" (1 Corinthians 7:14). The word sanctified means *set apart*. It is as if the unbelieving husband is set apart for special treatment by the Holy Spirit through his exposure to the believer's life. He is forced to think about the gospel because his wife's Christian life is such a part of his life.

The apostle Peter recommended the same strategy. "Wives, in the same way be submissive to your husbands so that, if any of them do not believe the word, they may be won over without words by the behavior of their wives" (1 Peter 3:1).

This concept has application beyond marriage; in any relationship where a Christian so lives that God's Spirit has an avenue into an unbeliever's life, the same "setting apart" or sanctification can take place.

Why Relational Evangelism Works

Why do people respond so positively to the gospel as it travels through these networks of relationships? The Institute for American Church Growth has suggested several reasons.

1. *Relational evangelism provides a natural network for sharing the good news.* The new Christian who has discovered the joy of salvation is eager to tell others, and it is natural that he will want to share this new freedom and joy with those who are closest to him.

2. *Relational evangelism focuses on friends and acquaintances who are receptive.* There is quite a difference between hearing the witness of a close, trusted friend whom you care about and hearing a "religious presentation" from a stranger.

3. *Relational evangelism allows for an unhurried, natural sharing of God's love.* One's witness is not squeezed into a short visit or intense presentation. Being a witness to the life-changing effects of God's love over a period of weeks, months, or even years allows unsaved friends and relatives time to consider the gospel message.

4. *Relational evangelism provides a natural support system.* The new convert's Christian friend is someone motivated to love, care for, and nurture them. The new Christian is not left alone.

5. *Relational evangelism results in the effective assimilation of new converts into the church.* It is natural for the new Christian to begin attending church where his or her friend or family member belongs. This makes it much easier to become associated with other Christians.

6. *Relational evangelism produces continually enlarging net-*

works of new contacts. Each person reached has his own network of relationships. New Christians tend to have more non-Christian in their circle of contacts because, over the years, a Christian's circle of friends becomes increasingly Christian.

What Your Class Can Do

Following are several ways you and your adults can work toward reaching lost friends and relatives.

■ *Develop a vision and concern for the lost.* The more we study the Word and pray the greater our spiritual conviction to reach the lost becomes. A result of your teaching should be adults with a vision and concern to reach the lost.

■ *Train adults to share their faith* with friends and relatives in simple, everyday language. Their close contacts comprise your extended congregation—casual attendees, visitors, and those whom the church members can influence because of their relationships.

■ *Select an evangelism coordinator* to focus the class' attention on outreach. This person would plan and coordinate special outreach events and emphases.

■ *Encourage students to bring unchurched friends to class.* Sunday school is a good place to bring people for their first exposure to the church. Most will find the informal class time less threatening and less foreign than the corporate worship service. Encourage adults to testify to the help they have found in the teaching and the fellowship of their Sunday school class.

■ *Select a hospitality coordinator* to ensure that visitors feel comfortable and welcome. Hospitality cannot be taken for granted. One person should have the responsibility to see that this is being done during and after the class.

■ *Train class members to be courteous and open to new people.* Selecting a hospitality coordinator does not absolve class members from the biblical obligation of hospitality. Each class member may "feel" hospitable toward a visitor or new member, but expressing those feelings in tangible, practical ways is what counts. Train your adults to greet visitors and to begin conversation.

■ *Lead individuals to Christ during the class session.* Teachers have a tendency to leave evangelism to the pastor in the morning service. But the classroom is a good setting for evangelism. It can be a more informal and personal setting than a large auditorium. If class members have been active in building friendships with a new person, their presence will be perceived as supportive rather than threatening.

■ *Encourage class members to submit the names* of unsaved family, friends, work associates, and neighbors. Encourage prayer for them. Don't underestimate what the Holy Spirit can do to reach someone who has been the target of concerted, heartfelt prayer. This, along with sincere overtures of friendship from class members, is a strategy that works.

EDUCATIONAL EVANGELISM

We turn now to how the adult Christian education ministries of the church can be better oriented to evangelism and outreach. This might be termed *educational evangelism.*

The Early Church enjoyed "the favor of all the people. And the Lord added to their number daily those who were being saved" (Acts 2:47). Basic to the community's perception of these early believers was their compassion and caring. They fed the hungry, healed the sick, shared possessions, and devoted themselves to teaching and fellowship. People are drawn to a caring church.

What needs exist in your community? What problems could your adult Sunday school class address? Classes that help meet the social, emotional, and spiritual needs of singles will have single Nathanaels coming to visit. Classes established to meet the needs of the newly married and/or new parents will have their share of Nathanaels also.

What about new converts or elderly adults? Does your church reach out to these special groups? What about extension ministries? Adult classes can be set up to meet regularly at locations and times better suited to the groups you are trying to reach. Many institutions, such as nursing homes, hospitals, and prisons, allow churches to hold devotional services. People who work Sunday mornings could meet at a more suitable time.

Analyze your ministry area as the first step to reach your community. Your ministry area refers to everyone who lives within either a 20-mile or 20-minute radius of the church building. However, it might also be defined as an area subgroup based on age, ethnic or cultural background, language, family status (such as single-parent families), and economic status.

Local libraries and city government agencies (such as your Department for Community Development) are the best sources for community demographic information. Ask for the census tract information for your community; this will report U.S. Census statistics for the various neighborhoods that comprise your community. This information will help your adult Christian education program become more community conscious and more responsive to adult needs. One of the great strengths of Sunday school is its ability to quickly form classes that focus on the needs of a particular group.

ADULT CHRISTIAN EDUCATION OUTREACH IDEAS

Develop Classes For People In Transition

A well-tested principle of church growth is that unchurched people are most responsive to a change in life-style, such as becoming a Christian during periods of life transition. A transition period is a span of time in which an individual's normal everyday behavior is disrupted by some irregular event that produces pain, discomfort, crisis, or change. These would include marriage, becoming a parent, losing a job, death or divorce of a spouse, moving to a new community, retirement or other such events. People in personally stable situations are not as open to radical departures from their established life-styles.

Plan "Entry" Level Events

Entry level events are designed to ease an unchurched person's first contact with the church. These special events include concerts, picnics, sight-seeing outings, workdays at the church, special seminars, and father-son or mother-daughter banquets. Unchurched adults who resist attending Sunday functions may come to events like these. Once contact is made and some relationships built, they may be more receptive to invitations to attend other functions and ministries of the church, such as Sunday school classes or the worship service.

Utilize New Converts

Newly converted adults are an important asset in reaching the adult community. They are nearly always enthusiastic about their new life in Christ; and their motivation needs to be tapped while it is high. There should be two primary goals for helping newly converted adults.

First, help them find a place within the church. Look at their natural abilities, and help them discover their spiritual gifts. God places *every* believer into a meaningful and productive place within the church. Involve new believers whenever possible; not only is this important to their self-esteem as new children of God, the church also benefits from their contribution.

Second, encourage and train newly converted adults to share their faith. New converts are often effective soul winners. They still have friends who are far from contact with the church. As time passes and friendships develop within the church the new convert releases his contact with those from his old life. This is normal because he feels comfortable with other Christians. Unfortunately, over time, Christians become increasingly insulated from contact with other adults who need to hear the gospel. So help new Christians share their faith while their motivation and contact with the unsaved are both high.

Increase Visibility In The Community

"He who has a thing to sell and goes and whispers in a well, is not so apt to get the dollars as he who climbs a tree and hollers." This humorous little saying has a great deal of application to the church as well as to business. We are in the business of winning people to Christ and bringing them into His fellowship. We should never forget that the wonderful truths of Scripture, that we sometimes take for granted, are the Bread of Life to a world dying of spiritual hunger.

Identify the Christian education ministries of your church that might appeal to the unchurched. What classes, courses, or seminars address needs within your community. Develop means of advertising what you can offer to your community. Advertise in the newspaper, but not on the religious page since most unchurched adults pay little attention to it. Consider public service announcements on local TV or radio stations.

Pray For The Unreached in Your Social Networks

"Unless the Lord builds the house, its builders labor in vain" (Psalms 127:1). The Church is God's means of reaching a lost world. Yet we cannot do the job without His supernatural enablement and direction. We find this power in prayer. Constant earnest prayer is vital in adult Sunday school growth. We should not give vague utterances for the lost of the world, but sincere petitions for specific individuals. As your adults pray for unsaved friends and acquaintances, their efforts to share their faith will result in the conversions.

Assimilating Newcomers Into the Adult Class

13

How many visitors have entered your classroom in the last two years? A review of class records may surprise you. We don't always appreciate the number of people who cycle through in that time. Too often they come in the front door only to slip unnoticed out the back door. By giving consistent and careful attention to visitors your class can grow.

Sunday school is the most effective ministry for assimilating people into the church. It's the only ministry of the church that can provide small-group attention to every individual, regardless of age, sex, or circumstance in life. But assimilation and incorporation are not automatic. Important questions must be faced. How do we make visitors feel comfortable? How can we ensure they leave with a positive experience and with the intention of returning? And, when they return how do we keep them coming? These are the subjects of this chapter.

WHAT IS ASSIMILATION?

"Assimilation is the process; incorporation is the goal."[35] Assimilation is everything your class does, both consciously and unconsciously, to make new people a part of the fellowship and life of the class. When done well, assimilation leads to incorporation, that is, people becoming integral members of the group.

Sociologists know that long-established groups can easily become closed. The longer a group has been together, the more difficult it is for outsiders to join. This is because members become closely linked by the traditions and common experiences they share. Newcomers do not share these and cannot identify with the group.

Few adults would consciously be impolite to new people. Unfortunately, groups sometimes unconsciously shut them out. Is it possible your class is so close-knit that it cannot grow? How open is your class to newcomers? A guest unrecognized, a handshake or a smile denied, a conversation unopened, a complimentary lesson-sheet denied all make visitors feel uncomfortable and unwelcome. Make your adults aware of this problem, promote an incorporation mentality within the class.

THE FRIENDSHIP FACTOR

Friendship links are an important factor in joining new people to a church or a Sunday school class. The more links a person has the more likely they will remain in the church. This was confirmed in one research study that compared 50 new class members still active 6 months after joining with 50 new members who were not active after 6 months. The new members who stayed had made more than seven new friends, those who dropped out had made less than two.[36]

We assume the primary function of the Sunday school is to teach the Bible. While education is certainly a major goal of the teacher, the primary factors that affect most people's continued attendance are relationships with others, their sense of belonging and social fellowship. Unless we give attention to these matters, Christian education will not be effective.

It is important to remember, however, that friendliness is not the same as assimilation. A visitor may feel your class is friendly, but still feel he cannot penetrate the social group and truly belong even after several weeks of attendance. It is not uncommon for classes to receive newcomers into the *membership circle* and yet unconsciously deny them access to the *fellowship circle*. So the question is not, "Is my class friendly?" but rather "What is my class doing to help visitors feel they belong?"

WHAT THE TEACHER CAN DO

While you cannot expect to retain every visitor, there are several things you can do to ensure the visitor leaves with a positive experience—and with the intention of returning. Here are some thoughts on hospitality and making visitors feel welcomed.

Arrive Early

Arrive early enough to personally greet every adult who walks through your door. Everyone appreciates a handshake and friendly greeting. Visitors and regulars alike need to know you are interested in them, and that you see them as more than just a number on the attendance report. In larger classes it may be physically impossible to personally greet every person. In this case, train personable members of your class to be official greeters.

Get Their Name Straight

Be sure to get the visitor's name straight. Taking time to get the proper spelling and pronunciation will tell a visitor you care about them. It should be standard procedure to have them fill in an information card with name, address, phone number, and other information helpful for follow up. Use their name several times as you speak to them. People love to hear their own name and will respond well to you.

Make Some Personal Introductions

Many classes formally introduce visitors at the start of the lesson. Be careful about publicly spotlighting visitors, such as making them stand. Surveys have shown that most visitors do **not** enjoy it. The trend seems to be toward more casual and nonthreatening assimilation techniques.

Before the teaching session begins, informally introduce the visitor to several individuals in the class. If possible, connect them with people of similar age, occupation, or interests. The more points of commonality the more comfortable the visitor will feel. They are more likely to return if they can look forward to seeing people they know. It is more effective to have visitors get to know a few members well than it is to have them formally stand before everyone in the class.

Train Regulars in Hospitality

Encourage class members to be open to new people. You may find it worthwhile to teach friendship skills—how to greet visitors and begin conversations. Class members may *feel* hospitable toward new people but not know how to *manifest* that hospitality in comfortable ways; and demonstrating those feelings in practical ways is what counts. Some members may want to consider a ministry of inviting visitors to sit with them during the worship service, or inviting them home or to a restaurant for dinner following the service. Visitors will be pleasantly impressed by such sincere invitations even if they decline the offer.

HOW TO IMPROVE ASSIMILATION

Select a Hospitality Coordinator

Hospitality should not be taken for granted, it is too easily overlooked. When everyone is responsible for hospitality (as they should be), everyone thinks someone else will do it. When one person has the *assigned* responsibility to coordinate hospitality it will not be neglected. The hospitality coordinator, or his coworkers, should welcome everyone as they enter the classroom, especially visitors. They can get the name, the address and the phone number of visitors, lead them to the refreshments, and introduce them to some class members.

Provide Informal Fellowship Time

Consider having a time of informal fellowship prior to the teaching session. This is an opportunity for adults to greet one another, share news, and simply enjoy social interaction. Adults always appreciate coffee, juice, and donuts served at this time;

it is also another motivation for the tardy to arrive on time. These 15 minutes of fellowship each week will do much to strengthen the class. It will help develop a sense of class identity and camaraderie. It is also helps visitors feel relaxed and allows the teacher or hospitality worker to introduce them to some people.

Provide Name Tags for Everyone

Traditionally, churches have identified visitors by some visible means. Visitors have been forced to stand publicly and tell about themselves, wear a flower or ribbon, or in some other way embarrass themselves. The majority of visitors feel uncomfortably conspicuous just being there. They don't want to feel marked as some kind of target.

Some classes, especially larger ones with frequent visitors, have *everyone* wear a name tag. This is done as a courtesy to visitors who may feel overwhelmed in a crowd of nameless strangers. It is easier to address someone when you can see their name. Regular members will also find it easier to converse and enlarge their circle of acquaintances, not to mention sparing them those desperate moments of panic when memory lapse steals someone's name. Visitors can still be recognized by having name tags with a different colored border.

Create a "Meet Our Class" Bulletin Board

Consider putting up a special bulletin board with photographs and names of all the individuals or couples who attend regularly. These pictures could be taken annually or semiannually at a class social event. If you have a one-hour photo service nearby, have two prints made that night. Use one print for the bulletin board, and return the other to the student(s). As adults join the class add them to the board. Having faces and names together on the board will help old-timers and newcomers alike.

Establish A New Member Tracking Committee

This committee monitors the first-year progress of newcomers to the class. This committee, composed of the teacher and selected class members, would be responsible to update student information files, watch attendance habits for signs of dropping out, help give new people opportunities to make contacts and establish friendships, and generally ensure the class is open to accept them. Some possible names for this committee would be the Care Committee or Lifeline Committee.[37]

Conduct "Where Did We Go Wrong" Interviews

Interview once-active but now inactive people in your community to find out why they dropped out. Without appearing to pressure them to return, simply state you are interested in improving your incorporation of new people. Tell them you would appreciate their honest and straight-forward statements and suggestions. Some people may be uncomfortable with this face-to-face encounter, in which case simply leave a form that they can fill in and return by mail. In many cases, reasons will be given for which the class has no responsibility; but occasionally someone's comment may suggest the class could have done more to assimilate them into the class. Don't be offended by their comments. Don't be defensive or try to rationalize class member's behavior. Simply accept their observations and thank them for cooperating. The class leadership should review and discuss the findings of this survey and plan for ways to better meet the needs of visitors to the class. This kind of analysis may be painful, but it will provide insights that might not otherwise be found.

KEEP ACCURATE RECORDS

Maintaining proper records is an underrated ministry of the Sunday school. The problem in most cases is that records are only kept and not used. Records can do much more than plot fluctuating attendance. Records are essential to ministry. Although worship service attendance is usually larger than Sunday school attendance, Sunday school records still provide the most accurate account of those present.

One of the first signs that a person is feeling frustrated or having a spiritual problem is irregular attendance. This makes the Sunday school class ideally suited among ministries in the church for the continued observation of an individual's needs. A Sunday school class is also best equipped to discover problems and take responsive measures before they become overwhelming and result in the person's leaving.

Records can help a teacher know students individually. A wise teacher will keep an information file on each student containing name, address, telephone number, birthday, wedding anniversary, spouse's name, occupation, children's names, spiritual background, hobbies, interests, and talents. Some classes, especially large ones, circulate a sheet of paper among students once a quarter asking for this kind of information. This allows them to update records and begin files for new members.

You may want to transfer birthday and anniversary dates onto a large calendar at home. Week by week you can look at the calendar to see who will be celebrating a birthday or anniversary. Cards should be sent and recognition made in class. It means a great deal when a teacher remembers any special occasion in a student's life. Cards cost money, of course, but the money (whether your own or the class') will be well spent.

Records lay the groundwork for productive visitation and follow-up. When someone visits your church or class, is anyone responsible to get their name, address, and some personal information? Such records allow follow-up calls, letters or visits to be made. Knowing something about a visitor can help direct him to groups with similar backgrounds and interests allowing for effective assimilation and ministry.

Records can help large classes determine the demographic composition of active members as well as people who drop out of a class or adult program. What population groups are you having success reaching? With which groups are you unsuccessful? Are there similarities among people who have left the class or the church in the last year or two? Does this mean a new class should be started to target a special group that is having difficulty fitting in? For example, if a large number of divorced adults are visiting and then leaving the church it may mean a divorce recovery course might help minister to a real need and assimilate these people into the church. The same would be true if the records show the church is not reaching and keeping ethnic groups or new parents.

FOLLOW GOOD ENROLLMENT POLICIES

Encourage the enrollment of any adult, anytime, and anywhere as long as he agrees and does not attend another church or Sunday school. This preenrollment gives the adult an immediate identification with your class. When he makes his first visit, he will already be a class member. This enrollment procedure also makes the individual a good prospect because he already has indicated his interest by agreeing to enroll. You have a name, address, and commitment which you can follow-up with a welcome and encouragement to attend regularly.

Enrolling unchurched adults is possible only if they have been convinced that their participation will truly help them. This is why it is very important to plan elective courses that speak directly to the needs and interests of the adults you are trying to reach. Worship service visitors and church members who do not attend Sunday school should be assigned to an appropriate age-level class for follow-up.

For years, classes have dropped a person's name from the enrollment records if they reached three consecutive absences. The only thing this accomplished was to *clean* the rolls. This maintained a good-looking attendance percentage of enrollment, it also freed class leadership from the task of following-up on absentees. But dropping poor attenders from the roll is *not* good ministry policy.

Remove names from the roll only if they die, they request it, they move from the community, they regularly attend another Sunday school, or removal is approved by the Sunday school executive committee. When someone moves to another community he should be given a letter of introduction to give to his new pastor. Your pastor should also contact the pastor(s) in the person's new community so he can welcome him.

PRACTICE GOOD FOLLOW-UP PROCEDURES

Follow-up of visitors and absentees expresses concern. It says, "We want you to be a part of us." This kind of pastoral care requires good record keeping and a clear organization of responsibility. In smaller classes follow-up usually falls to the teacher. But whether another person handles follow-up or not, the teacher should be involved. Follow-up could be given to a volunteer or assigned to the class evangelism coordinator or hospitality coordinator. These helpers will not only lighten the teacher's workload, they will also make a favorable and lasting impression.

Your class or adult Sunday school should adopt the following guidelines or develop its own follow-up guidelines.

1. *Every first-time visitor should receive a personal letter, phone call, or visit within 48 hours.* These do not need to be lengthy. A short message of welcome and your commitment to minister to him is sufficient.

If you plan to visit, a brief phone call would be wise for several reasons. People are busy, and you might make several trips before finding them at home. Not only is calling ahead a courtesy, but it will also keep you from dropping in at the wrong time. People also like some warning to tidy up the homestead before you surprise them with a visit.

Shortly after my wife and I visited a Sunday school class after moving to town, we were visited by two class members. These ladies gave us a warm welcome along with literature about the class and the church. What most impressed us was the warm, freshly baked loaf of bread they brought with them. They explained it was symbolic of the class' desire to share Christ, the Bread of Life with us. This thoughtful (and delicious) gift was a novel approach that communicated a great deal to us about the friendliness of the class members.

2. *Teachers are expected to visit each pupil in his home to build relationships.* As the teacher, you are also viewed as the class leader. Your contact with students is important. They need to feel you know and care about them as individuals. These visits

help build and maintain the teacher-student relationship so vital for effective teaching.

3. *When a student is absent for a known reason (illness, vacation, etc.), a postcard or personal note may be sent.* A brief message expressing your prayer for a quick recovery, or your hope for a good vacation, for example, would be appropriate. This is especially effective in a large class where the student may feel that he is unnoticed and insignificant.

4. *If the absence is for an unknown reason, a phone call or a personal visit should be made.* This is not to scold them for being gone, but rather to let them know they were missed. Adults do not respond well to an overbearing, truant-officer approach to follow-up. Contacts should be natural, supportive, and positive.

5. *Follow-up to subsequent absences requires sensitivity to the person and the situation.* A personal visit or ongoing contact with an absentee is important and needs to communicate love and acceptance to the individual.

6. *The pastor or pastoral staff should be informed of situations that require a pastoral visit.* Anyone who makes a follow-up visit should understand he is part of the church's ministry team. Teamwork requires they communicate to the pastoral staff or other relevant leadership any time they learn of important situations in their contact's life or family situation.

7. *The Sunday school executive committee should constantly monitor absences to analyze trends and correct weaknesses.*

CONCLUSION

Welcoming visitors and assimilating newcomers is not easy. What *is* easy is gradually falling into neglect of this important work. Churches have traditionally spent a great deal of time, money, and effort to bring people in the front door of the church; and yet have failed to expend an equal effort to prevent their leaving through the back door. The church or Sunday school class that will make a conscious, disciplined commitment to work on assimilation will grow.

CHAPTER NOTES

[1] C. B. Eavey, *History of Christian Education* (Chicago: Moody Press, 1964), 78.

[2] Michael Lawson, *The Christian Educator's Handbook on Teaching* (Victor Books, 1988), 64–67.

[3] *Webster's Ninth New Collegiate Dictionary*, (1988).

[4] Malcolm S. Knowles, *The Modern Practice of Adult Education* (New York: Cambridge Press, 1980), 44-45.

[5] James DeBoy, *Getting Started in Adult Religious Education* (New York: Paulist Press, 1979), 75-79.

[6] K. Patricia Cross, *Adults As Learners* (San Francisco: Jossey-Bass Publishers, 1987), 146.

[7] Ibid., 82.

[8] Charles Sell, *Transition - The Stages of Adult Life* (Chicago: Moody Press, 1985), x.

[9] Knowles, 51.

[10] Sell, *Transition*, xxi.

[11] Gilbert A. Peterson, *The Christian Education of Adults* (Chicago: Moody Press, 1984), 80.

[12] Chris Caldwell, "Having To Deal With Transition." *Christian Single* (published by The Sunday School Board of the Southern Baptist Convention; Nashville, Tenn.).

[13] Jerry M. Stubblefield, *A Church Ministering to Adults* (Nashville, Tenn.: Broadman Press, 1986), 52.

[14] Gail Sheehy, *Passages-Predictable Crises of Adult Life* (New York: Bantam Books, 1976), 37-39.

[15] Ibid., 37

[16] Sharan B. Merriam and Trenton R. Ferro, *Handbook of Adult Religious Education*, ed. by Nancy Foltz (Birmingham, AL: Religious Education Press), 62.

[17] J. Gordon Chamberlin, quoted in *Adult Education in the Church*, Roy B. Zuck and Gene A Getz, editors (Chicago: Moody Press, 1970), 35.

[18] Terry Hershey, *Young Adult Ministry* (Loveland, Colo.: Group Books, 1986), 43.

[19] Ibid.

[20] Ibid., p 44.

[21] Robert J. Havighurst, *Developmental Tasks and Education* (New York: David McKay Company, Inc., 1972), 95-106.

[22] Vital Statistics of the United States 1982, Volume 3, Marriage and Divorce.

[23] Havighurst, 107-116.

[24] Bureau of the Census, SB-3-89, November, 1989.

[25] Peterson, 149.

[26] Ibid., 150.

[27] William Martin, *First Steps for Teachers* (Springfield, Mo.: Gospel Publishing House, 1984), 84,85.

[28] Ronald G. Held, *Learning Together* (Springfield, Mo.: Gospel Publishing House, 1976), 34.

[29] Donald L. Griggs, *Teaching Teachers to Teach* (Livermore, Calif.: Griggs Educational Service, 1974), 18,19.

[30] Perry G. Downs, "The Curriculum of Adult Education," in *The Christian Education of Adults*, ed., Gilbert Peterson (Chicago: Moody Press, 1984), 118-121.

[31] George Edgerly and Harold Crosby, *Strategies for Sunday School Growth* (Springfield, Mo: Gospel Publishing House, 1983), 83-84.

[32] Phillip B. Jones, *RD Digest* (Research Division, Home Mission Board, Southern Baptist Convention), February 1989.

[33] Ibid.

[34] Peterson, 64.

[35] Quoted from DIRECTIONS—the Assemblies of God resource for developing the Sunday school and related ministries. Available from the Sunday School Promotion & Training Department.

[36] Charles Arn, Donald McGavran and Win Arn *Growth—A New Vision for the Sunday School* (Pasadena, Calif.: Church Growth Press, 1980), 95.

[37] Ibid., 101.